Current Population Trends in the United States

Current Population Trends in the United States

George Sternlieb and
James W. Hughes

CENTER FOR URBAN POLICY RESEARCH

THE CENTER FOR URBAN POLICY RESEARCH
P.O. BOX 38
NEW BRUNSWICK, NEW JERSEY 08903

Cover Design by Francis G. Mullen

Copyright, 1978, Rutgers-The State University of New Jersey

All Rights Reserved.

Published in the United States of America by the Center for Urban Policy Research New Brunswick, New Jersey 08903

Manufactured in the United States of America

Library of Congress Cataloging in Publication Data

Sternlieb, George.
    Current population trends in the United States.

    Includes bibliographical references.
        1. United States—Population.   I. Hughes, James W., joint author.
    II. Title.
HB3505.S73   301.32'9'73   77-17420
ISBN 0-88285-053-9

Contents

Current Population Trends in the United States

1

Introduction

America's planners have a bent for the short run. Immediate exigencies and fast payback for current decisions tend to govern our thinking. Long-term basic shifts are given lip service, but all too often are assigned to the university for bloodless observation. Polite bows are made by the professional, both within and outside government, to the existence of these shifts. But this is far more ritual than vital. The time lag for profound social change is enormously costly, as witness the debate over which neighborhood school to close, or where the water for western growth nodes is to come from—and whether it can get there in time to avert disaster.

Beneath the surface of momentary issues are evolutionary tides whose long-term impact promises to dwarf the more visible problem areas of the postwar era. And one of the major forces of change in this context is the web of population dynamics and its evolving form and structure. From such diverse phenomena as the Gross National Product to land use and the sale of diapers, there are no significant areas of our lives—or developmental patterns—which are not deeply associated with this reality. And certainly never more so than at the present time.

The sweeping changes in the demographic profile of America have certainly not escaped the attention of the popular media. Abounding are ominous stories of an increased elderly population rapidly depleting the limited storechest of social security, with the burden of support soon to be thrust upon a hard-pressed younger generation. Equivalent tales indicate that clearance sales should be held on educational facilities and that a teacher's license is but a passport to functional obsolescence. Yet these concerns are very real and represent but a limited sample of the far-ranging consequences of the demographic changes that are underway.

THE BROADER OBJECTIVE

In the material presented here we have attempted to provide a concise overview of the basic data with which to analyze the major population trends of America as they have evolved in the recent past and as they promise to extend themselves in the short term future. The perspective is not one of the professional demographer, but rather that of the urban planner, concerned with the implications of the broader social and economic parameters of public policy-making and planning. As such, future directions and their consequences are of major import.

Fortunately, projections in the population domain, at least at the national scale, are far from being as obscure as is the case in many other areas. Unlike the pattern of future international relations, or of technological advance—both of which are subject to the idiosyncracies of individuals and the vagaries of events that are beyond precise definition—one can forecast with considerable reliability the number of women of childbearing years over the next decade and a half (though not the number of children which they will decide to bear), the size of the working age population for an even longer period (though not its labor force participation patterns), and a variety of other phenomena. Consequently, while prognostication is always hazardous, there are certain future population parameters that can be anticipated with some degree of confidence. In the same context, however, reasoned speculation is required for many others.

ORGANIZATIONAL PARTITIONS

Within the framework of a limited objective—a concise overview of recent population trends—it has been necessary to strictly limit and demarcate the scope of the subject matter considered. The range and richness of the data base are such that very difficult decisions regarding inclusion and exclusion were continually faced. Our goal is to provide the basic building blocks of data, and to suggest some preliminary implications. If the reader feels certain concerns have been slighted, it has certainly not been intentional. It is simply the result of our belief that more learned observers would have better facility for providing more definitive interpretations and analysis.

Seven major population phenomena have been isolated to serve as major organizational partitions:

1. The National Growth Deceleration
2. The Age Structure Evolution
3. Household Compositional Changes
4. Population and Labor Force Growth Patterns
5. Family and Employment Characteristics

6. Changing Spatial Distribution: Regional
7. Population Redistribution: Metropolitan, Nonmetropolitan, and Intrametropolitan

While to a certain extent each of these elements penetrates and has an impact on the remainder—interrelationships that we attempt to specify, where feasible—the separation is of analytical utility, providing useful and distinguishable focal points relevant to planners and public policymakers.

The analysis begins at the very general level of broad national growth trends and then focuses on two internal facets—age structure and household composition. Subsequently, attention is directed to the impact of these factors on the labor force, first in terms of individuals, and then in terms of the family unit. Finally, the spatial redistribution of America's citizenry is considered: both the evolving patterns and their linkage to the dynamics underlying the preceding population trendlines.

OVERVIEW OF THE ANALYSIS
The National Growth Deceleration

1. Population growth in the United States is decelerating markedly. From 1955 to 1960, the nation's population increased by 14.8 million people, or 9.0 percent. In contrast, the growth increment from 1970 to 1975 was 8.9 million people, or 4.4 percent. America's population increased by 2.2 million people during 1970, or 1.09 percent. During 1976, it increased by only 1.6 million people or .73 percent.

2. Population change is the consequence of two components—net natural increase (births minus deaths), and immigration. Key to the recent national growth experience has been the decline in the number of births.

3. The total fertility rate, the number of births a woman would expect to have through her childbearing years, stood at 1.76 in 1976, substantially below replacement level fertility (2.115) and far below the peak registered during the 1955 to 1959 period (3.690).

4. Unless there are sharp changes in the fertility rate in the immediate future, the growth rate over the next ten years will tend to replicate that attained in the first half of the 70's.

The Age Structure Evolution

1. Within the context of slower national growth, the size of specific age groups has and will vary sharply, reflecting present and past trends in the level of fertility.

2. The changes in age distribution tend to be dominated by three major phenomena.
   a. The post World War II baby boom has inserted a permanent but moving bulge into the nation's evolving age structure.
   b. The subsequent baby bust, the consequence of declining fertility after 1957, is characterized by contracting age cohorts in contrast to the expansions caused by the baby boom.
   c. The ranks of the elderly, those 65 years of age and over, will continue to expand in size and social significance.

3. From 1970 to 1976, when the nation's total population increased by 10.2 million, these groups experienced the following changes:
    a. The population between the ages of 18 to 34 years, the baby boom progeny, increased by 10.2 million people, equivalent to the total national growth increment.
    b. Concurrently, there was a decline of 4.5 million people 17 years of age and under, the result of the baby bust. This was reflected by an elementary school enrollment decline of 4.2 million pupils.
    c. The elderly population increased by 2.8 million people. The median age of America's population, after declining to 27.9 years in 1970, increased to 29.0 years in 1976.

4. These three groups will also dominate the age structure changes through 1985.
    a. The baby boom, as it filters into the 25 to 44 years of age category, will increase the size of the latter by 16.0 million people between 1976 and 1985.
    b. The maturing baby bust will begin to be reflected in the 18 to 24 years of age category, which will decline by 1.6 million people between 1980 and 1985, as well as in the 5 to 17 year old age group, which will contract by about 6.4 million people between 1976 and 1985.
    c. Over the latter period, the number of individuals over 65 years of age will increase by 4.4 million people. By 1985, the median age of America's populace will exceed 31.5 years.

5. Blacks and other races will increase as a percent of the total population, moving from 12.4 percent in 1970 to 14.4 percent in 1985. Among the younger age groups, their proportional representation will be even greater.

Household Compositional Changes

1. Declining fertility, slower national growth, and the formation of independent households by the maturing baby boom, all contribute to marked changes in the composition of America's households.

2. A key indicator of the transformation underway is the household size parameter, which has shifted from 3.33 persons in 1960 to 2.89 persons in 1976.

3. Contributing to this change are declining marriage rates and soaring divorce rates, as well as the increasing prevelance of childless married women. In 1960, 15.0 percent of America's married women 44 years of age and under were childless; by 1976, the equivalent was 18.8 percent.

4. As a result, the nation's household formats are visibly changing.
    a. Traditional husband-wife families accounted for 74.3 percent of all households in 1960; by 1976, they accounted for only 64.9 percent. Their rate of growth from 1970 to 1976, 5.7 percent, was the slowest of any household configuration.
    b. Households comprising a single individual have increased their proportional share from 13.1 percent in 1960 to 20.6 percent in 1976. Their growth rate from 1970 to 1976 was 38.1 percent.
    c. The fastest growing household type is composed of primary individuals with nonrelatives present. Their 1970 to 1976 growth rate exceeded 67 percent; much of the growth has been in two person households comprising unrelated individuals of the opposite sex.

d. Also expanding rapidly are female-headed families (no husband present). This group had a 1970 to 1976 growth rate of 33.4 percent, six times as fast as traditional husband-wife families.

Population and Labor Force Growth Patterns

1. Interrelated with each of the preceding developments are changing patterns of labor force participation. While the noninstitutional working age population of the United States increased by 46.3 percent from 1950 to 1976, the civilian labor force increased by 52.3 percent.

2. At the same time, the female component of the civilian labor force expanded by 108.9 percent. The labor force participation rate of women increased from 33.9 percent in 1950 to 47.2 percent in 1976.

3. Significantly, the male component of the labor force actually trailed population growth, increasing by only 28.6 percent from 1950 to 1976.

Family and Employment Characteristics

1. The traditional husband-wife family represents a shrinking proportion of America's total households; it also incorporates a growing proportion of working wives.

2. The number of employed husbands increased by 23.0 percent between 1947 and 1976; the number of working wives expanded by 208.0 percent. The labor force participation rate of wives increased from 23.8 percent in 1950 to 44.4 percent in 1975. Over this same time period, the proportion of families with two workers or more increased from 36.1 percent to 48.7 percent.

3. In 1975, only 34 percent of all husband-wife families were represented in the labor force solely by the husband; by contrast 41 percent had both the husband and wife in the labor force.

4. Children are *positively* correlated with the labor force participation of wives. Married women (husband present) with school age children had a labor force participation rate of 53.7 percent in 1976, compared to 28.3 percent in 1950.

5. As a consequence of these phenomena, the nation's median family income increased by 313.3 percent from 1950 to 1975; in contrast, average weekly earnings expanded by only 209.4 percent.

6. Families with wives in the paid labor force had a median family income of $16,928 in 1974; families with wives not in the paid labor force had an equivalent income of $12,082.

Changing Spatial Distribution: Regional

1. The declining rates of fertility and net natural increase leave migration in a more prominent role in determining local population growth. As a matter of individual decisionmaking, the southern and western parts of the nation have emerged as residential environments of choice.

2. From 1950 to 1975, the Northeast and North Central Regions secured decreasing shares of declining national growth. In contrast, the South and West have steadily increased their share, from 55.9 percent in the 1950 to 1960 period, to 61.0 percent the ensuing 10 years, and to 86.0 percent in the 1970 to 1976 period.

6

3. The acceleration after 1970 is accentuated by the migration experience. From 1970 to 1975, the South and West secured 4 million net immigrants, while the Northeast and North Central states experienced a net outmigration of 1.5 million people.

Metropolitan-Nonmetropolitan Shifts

1. Metropolitan areas have long been recognized as the dominant population growth poles in America. However a marked transformation occurred after 1970. From 1970 to 1976, the nation's metropolitan areas experienced a population growth rate of 4.0 percent. Concurrently, nonmetropolitan areas had an 8.2 percent population increase.

2. This reversal was led by the large metropolitan areas of the Northeast and North Central states, which experienced both net outmigration and absolute population declines in the post-1970 period.

Intra-Metropolitan Shifts

1. From 1970 to 1976 America's central cities in total experienced absolute population losses for the first time, losing 3.4 percent or 2.1 million individuals. In contrast, the same central cities had a 6.5 percent increase in population from 1960 to 1970.

2. The net loss of whites in the central cities from 1970 to 1976 (3.7 million) was not compensated by black population increases (1.5 million).

3. Black suburbanization is gaining substantial momentum. From 1970 to 1976, the number of blacks residing in suburbia increased by 36.3 percent.

The Prominent Issues

This web of changes raises a number of issues germain to planning and public policymaking.

1. The maturation of the baby boom products into their working age years, in conjunction with the rapid accession of women into the labor force, has and will continue to place significant stress on the American economy.

2. The housing market implications attendant to the households formed by the baby boom are problematical. As this group ages to between 25 and 34 years, the traditional scenario would imply single family home purchases. Yet the emerging household configurations indicate a logic for smaller units. The ultimate desires and economic capacities have yet to be defined.

3. The shrinking age cohorts of the baby bust raise the question of excess capacities of many public facilities and services. Presently impacting the nation's elementary school systems, these cohorts will create similar problems to afflict higher level educational institutions. Contraction may become an important entry into the planner's lexicon.

4. Such problems will be both mitigated and aggravated by regional and metropolitan population shifts; areas of declining population will experience even more traumatic underutilization while growth territories may have to replicate facilities that are being vacated elsewhere.

5. As the baby bust individuals enter their working age years in the future, it is

entirely possible that a labor market transformation will occur—to one of labor shortages—presenting unique opportunities for the nation's minority groups.

6. The increasing representation of the elderly in American society will have profound repercussions—economic, political, and social.

2

The National Growth Deceleration

The most dominant and persisting trait of America's evolving demographic profile during the past twenty years has been the deceleration of the population growth rate. Is it a short term aberration? Or is it continually gaining validity as a long term trendline?[1] What are the contours of the basic evolution?

Exhibit 1 presents the total population estimates of the United States from 1950 to 1975 by five-year intervals, as well as the changes for each of these periods.[2] Over the entire twenty-five-year time span, the population of the nation increased by more than 61 million people—more than the total population of France, equivalent to the total population of West Germany or 55 percent of the total population of Japan.[3] The manifestations of this growth are evident at every hand—from the enormous sweep of suburbia to the burgeoning restaurant industry.

But the expansion has been far from constant. As detailed at the bottom of the Exhibit 1, the rate of growth has declined from the 1955 to 1960 peak of 9.0 percent to the 1970 to 1975 rate of 4.4 percent. Between these two periods, the decline both in the rate of growth and the absolute increment has been consistent and sustained. Indeed, the increase of the 1970 to 1975 period was 5.9 million people less than that experienced from 1955 to 1960.

The pattern is highlighted as the present decade is examined in more detail. Exhibit 2 presents the current annual estimates of the population of the United States from 1970 to 1977. Despite an ever increasing base, the annual growth increment has been reduced from 2.2 million people in 1970 to 1.6 million in 1976. However, there are indeed fluctuations in these annual estimates,

EXHIBIT 1
ESTIMATES OF THE POPULATION OF THE UNITED STATES:
JANUARY 1, 1950 TO JANUARY 1, 1975
(numbers in thousands)

Population Level

Year	Population Estimate[1]
1950	151,135
1955	164,588
1960	179,386
1965	193,223
1970	203,849
1975	212,748

Population Change

Period	Number	Percent
1950–1955	13,453	8.9
1955–1960	14,798	9.0
1960–1965	13,837	7.7
1965–1970	10,626	5.6
1970–1975	8,899	4.4

NOTE: 1. Total population, including Armed Forces overseas.

SOURCES: U.S. Bureau of the Census, *Statistical Abstract of the United States:1975* (Washington, D.C.: U.S. Government Printing Office, 1975), p. 11; U.S. Bureau of the Census, *Current Population Reports,* Series P-20, No. 307, "Population Profile of the United States:1976" (Washington, D.C.: U.S. Government Printing Office, April 1977).

some of which have been caused by unforeseen events—i.e., about 130,000 Vietnamese refugees entered the country in 1975.[4]

Providing the key to the variations shown in Exhibit 2 are three factors—births, deaths and immigration—that comprise the basic causal components of population change. The first itself is the consequence of not only the rate of fertility (the number of births that a woman would have in her lifetime, if, at each year of age, she experienced the birth rate occurring in the specified year), but also the number of women of childbearing age, i.e., given equivalent fertility rates, a base of 1,000 women of a given age distribution will produce fewer children than a base of 1,100 women. Nonetheless, fertility is a telling indicator by itself and deserves immediate attention.[5]

EXHIBIT 2
ESTIMATES OF THE POPULATION OF THE UNITED STATES, AND ANNUAL
INCREASE: JANUARY 1, 1970 TO JANUARY 1, 1977
(numbers in thousands)

Year	Population Estimate[1]
1970	203,849
1971	206,076
1972	208,088
1973	209,711
1974	211,207
1975	212,748
1976	214,435
1977	215,998

Period	Absolute Increase	Percent Increase
1970	2,227	1.09
1971	2,012	0.98
1972	1,623	0.78
1973	1,496	0.71
1974	1,541	0.73
1975	1,687	0.79
1976	1,563	0.73

NOTE: 1. Total population, including Armed Forces overseas.

SOURCE: U.S. Bureau of the Census, *Current Population Reports,* Series P-20, No.
307, "Population Profile of the United States:1976" (Washington, D.C.: U.S.
Government Printing Office, April 1977).

FERTILITY RATES

Exhibit 3 presents one of the key touchstones of the demographers' art
form, indicating the trends in fertility over the past two and one-half decades.
(As a point of reference, a total fertility rate of 2.115 represents "replacement
level" fertility for the total population under current mortality conditions.) In
the 1950 to 1954 period, the total rate was at the 3.337 level, i.e., 3,337 children
would be born per 1,000 women. The peak of modern times was experienced in
the 1955 to 1959 period when the rate increased to 3.690. Since that time, however, it has decreased very sharply, with the 1970 to 1974 average fertility rate
standing at 2.106, a level just below the replacement threshold.

EXHIBIT 3
TOTAL FERTILITY RATE: 1950 TO 1974 BY FIVE-YEAR
PERIODS AND 1970 TO 1976 BY YEAR

Period	Total Fertility Rate[1]
1950–1954	3.337
1955–1959	3.690
1960–1964	3.459
1965–1969	2.636
1970–1974	2.106
Year	
1970	2.480
1971	2.275
1972	2.022
1973	1.896
1974	1.857
1975	1.799
1976	1.760

NOTE: 1. The fertility rate indicates how many births a woman would have by the end of her childbearing years if, during her entire reproductive period, she were to experience the age-specific birth rates for the given period.

SOURCE: U.S. Bureau of the Census, *Current Population Reports,* Series P-20, No. 307, "Population Profile of the United States:1976" (Washington, D.C.: U.S. Government Printing Office, April 1977).

Just how precipitous this decline has been is revealed in the latter half of Exhibit 3, where the rate attendant to each individual year of the 1970s is presented. As would be expected, there appears to be an inexorable and steady decline in each of these benchmarks. Indeed, the 1.760 rate of 1976 is 29 percent less than the 2.480 rate of 1970, and almost 17 percent below the replacement level rate.

This does not mean, however, that the population of the United States, even without immigration, faces imminent decline; given the increasing number of women of childbearing age, the immediate prospect is for sustained net natural increases (births minus deaths) in the nation's total population. But it does indicate that over a longer period of time, if the present fertility rate persists, the future population of the United States, sans immigration, will be

EXHIBIT 4

ESTIMATES OF THE COMPONENTS OF POPULATION CHANGE FOR THE UNITED STATES:
JANUARY 1, 1970 TO JANUARY 1, 1977
(numbers in thousands)

Year	Population at Beginning of Period[1]	Total Increase[2]	Natural Increase			Net Civilian Immigration
			Net	Births	Deaths	
1970	203,849	2,227	1,812	3,739	1,927	438
1971	206,076	2,012	1,626	3,556	1,930	387
1972	208,088	1,623	1,293	3,258	1,965	325
1973	209,711	1,496	1,163	3,137	1,974	331
1974	211,207	1,541	1,225	3,160	1,935	316
1975	212,748	1,687	1,238	3,149	1,911	450[3]
1976	214,435	1,563	1,249	3,163	1,914	314
1977	215,118	—	—	—	—	—

NOTES:
1. Total population, including Armed Forces overseas.
2. Includes estimates of admissions into and discharges from the Armed Forces overseas, and for 1970 includes error of closure between censuses.
3. Includes about 130,000 Vietnamese refugees who entered the United States during 1975.

SOURCE: U.S. Burdeau of the Census, *Current Population Reports*, Series P-20, No. 307, "Population Profile of the United States:1976" (Washington, D.C.: U.S. Government Printing Office, April 1977).

reduced—and significantly. This future possibility will be returned to later, but to highlight the present situation a summary of the detailed components of population change is necessary.

THE COMPONENTS OF POPULATION CHANGE

As shown in Exhibit 4, given the continual decrease in the fertility rate over the 1970 to 1976 period, the net natural increase declined from 1.8 million people in 1970 to below 1.2 million people in 1973, but then proceeded to rise very slowly above the 1.2 million person plateau between 1973 and 1976. The same pattern is evident in the total number of births, with an apparent bottoming out in 1973. As will be considered in the following section, these slight upward shifts are a consequence of the changing age structure of the United States. Nonetheless, the significance of the number of births in 1976 (3.163 million) is emphasized by the magnitude of those recorded at the 1957 peak (4.308 million): in excess of 1.1 million more births occurred in 1957 than in 1976.

At the same time, with the exception of the unique Vietnamese incursion of 1975, net civilian immigration has tended to shrink over time, declining from 438,000 in 1970 to 314,000 in 1976. Unfortunately, the changing dimensions of illegal immigration into the United States are not captured by the standard data accounts. Current estimates of the absolute size of this population vary enormously, from relatively trivial numbers to above 10,000,000 people. The net annual additions to such purported bases are the subject of even hazier estimates. Nonetheless, this is a significant phenomenon and will be returned to in the discussion of population and the labor force.

THE FUTURE

Given the pattern of steadily decreasing rates of population increase over the past twenty years and the consistent decline in the rate of fertility during the last decade, what are the short-term expectations for national population growth? Variations in the future will continue to be a function of the fertility rate and the number of women of childbearing age, assuming that mortality rates and immigration levels do not change significantly. As will be explored subsequently, the number of women of child bearing age will be increasing significantly over the next decade—the products of the maturation of the post-World War II baby boom—making it possible for the number of births to increase even in the context of reduced fertility. Additionally, the sheer size of the fertile cohorts could amplify any positive fertility rate fluctuations into much larger population growth consequences.

The Census Bureau's most recent projection sets comprise three different series, each reflecting different assumptions about the rate of fertility.[6] These rates are assumed to move toward the following levels:

Series I   2.7
Series II 2.1
Series III 1.7

Additionally, all assume a slight improvement in mortality and an annual net immigration of 400,000 people.

Exhibit 5 presents the 1980 and 1985 projections, as well as the shifts experienced from 1970 to 1975. The 1975 to 1980 anticipated growth is between 7.2 million and 10.5 million people, although the upper bound is probably unrealistic in light of the fertility rate experience already recorded in the early stages of this period. The most likely expectation is probably an increase similar to, or somewhat below, the 8.6 million increase demonstrated in the 1970 to 1975 period, i.e., the Series II and III projections.

The effects of differential fertility rates will tend to pyramid as the span of time lengthens. Hence from 1980 to 1985, the range of absolute increase broadens to between 8 million and 15 million people. If the fertility rate experiences a sharp upsurge—a probability that will be subsequently entertained—the total United States population will approach the 239 million person level by 1985; if the present rate is maintained, the population projection would approach 229 million. While the implications of these alternative paths are significant—for example, consideration of the influence each of these paths will have on housing formats in the immediate future and the nation's educational infrastructure in a slightly longer range framework—America's future economic and social life will still be dominated by the extant population. This situation should be evident as we examine the internal composition of the nation's populace—the age structure evolution.

SUMMARY

The issue of controlling and managing growth gained the center stage of the planning profession in the decade of the 1970s. Following two decades of growth aspirations, a growing number of the nation's suburbs, in concert with broader national movements, began to entertain the wisdom of no-growth. In an unusual convergence of desire and reality, America's demographic evolution matched this shift with a long-term decline in the rate of population increase.

1. For each successive five year interval over the past twenty year period (1955 to 1975), both the absolute population growth increment of the United States, and the rate of increase, declined significantly.

2. From 1970 to 1975, the nation's population increased by 8.9 million people (4.4 percent). The equivalent growth for the 1955 to 1960 period was 14.8 million (9.0 percent).

EXHIBIT 5

ESTIMATED AND PROJECTED POPULATION OF THE UNITED STATES: JULY 1, 1970 TO JULY 1, 1985[1]

(numbers in thousands)

	1970	1975	Change 1970–1975		1980	Change 1975–1980		1985	Change 1980–1985	
			Number	Percent		Number	Percent		Number	Percent
Population	204,878	213,540	8,662	4.2	I. 224,066	10,526	4.9	238,878	14,812	6.6
					II. 222,159	8,619	4.0	232,880	10,721	4.8
					III. 220,732	7,192	3.4	228,879	8,147	3.7

NOTES: 1. Includes Armed Forces overseas.

2. The projections were prepared using the "cohort-component" method and comprise three Series—I, II, and III. All assume a slight improvement in mortality, an annual net immigration of 400,000, and completed cohort fertility rates (i.e., average number of lifetime births per 1,000 women) that move toward the following levels: Series I—2,700; Series II—2,100; Series III—1,700.

SOURCE: U.S. Bureau of the Census Current Population Reports, Series P-25, No. 704, "Projections of the Population of the United States:1975 to 2050" (Washington, D.C.: U.S. Government Printing Office, July 1977).

3. For 1970, the annual total growth was 2.2 million people (1.09 percent). By 1976, the annual increment declined to 1.6 million people (0.73 percent). The nation's total population as of January 1, 1977 was estimated at 216 million people, compared to 204 million people in 1970.

4. Underlying this pervasive slowdown is the decline in the fertility rate, which in 1976 was at the 1.76 level, far below the replacement level threshold of 2.115.

5. The fertility rate is the most critical assumption determining future population estimates. The Census Bureau's Series III projection, which employs a fertility rate most closely approximating present reality, indicates that the total population of the United States in 1985 will approach 229 million, implying a growth increment somewhat smaller than the recent past, although the sharp increases in the number of women of childbearing age will have started to push the rate upward in the 1980s.

3

Age Structure Evolution

There are three major phenomena that have shaped the last twenty-five years and whose implications will be a basic part of the future: the baby boom, the baby bust, and the growth of the elderly population. The post-World War II baby boom was initiated in 1946 by an approximate 20 percent increase in the number of live births compared to that recorded in 1945. A steady increase in the annual number of births continued to 1957, the peak year of the postwar era. About 47 million children were born over a twelve year span, accounting for over 21 percent of the present 1977 population. It is this group that has inserted a permanent but moving bulge into America's age structure, flooding the nation's school systems in the 1950s and 1960s, its higher educational system in the 1960s and 1970s, and its job and housing markets in the 1970s.

The subsequent baby bust, by definition, is foreordained to trail in the wake of the baby boom as it matures through the country's age cohorts. While the latter produced 47 million children during the twelve year period from 1946 to 1957, the number of live births in the last twelve year period, 1965 to 1976, was only 41 million. Facilities and opportunities predicated on a larger predecessor population are now beginning to experience the initial stages of partial voids, a phenomenon that will be increasingly prevalent over the next decade.

Finally, the elderly—those sixty-five years of age and over—are continually increasing in number and significance. Their number has virtually doubled to 23 million people over the last twenty-five years, and now account for almost 11 percent of the nation's population total (as compared to 8.1 percent in 1950).

Each of these phenomena tends to dominate the age structure shifts that have taken place in the United States from 1950 to 1976, and will continue to dominate in the future. In the following analysis, these changes will be evaluated decade by decade; attempts will be made to draw correlations between these changes and recent social and economic events, and the implications for the short-term future will be reviewed.

THE 1950 TO 1960 PERIOD

The era of the baby boom is shown very clearly in the 1950 to 1960 data portrayed in Exhibit 6. In that decade, the population of the United States increased by 28.4 million people; of this increase, over 17.2 million were 17 years of age or under, accounting for 61 percent of the total growth. Indeed, a 13.3 million person increase was registered in the five to seventeen years of age cohort alone. It is this gathering bulge which already has been, and will be, basic to developmental patterns in the United States as a whole. Much of the shift to suburbia, and the attendant stress on educational plant development (as well as its complement, school financing problems) was a consequence of these incredible quanta.

But at the same time, a relatively low level of growth was experienced in the ranks of the eighteen to twenty-four years of age cohort, and an actual decline of 1.1 million people between the ages of twenty-five to thirty-four years was realized, reflecting the aftereffects of reduced Depression era birth rates. Given an expanding economy, these were years of great employment opportunities for the latter group, not the least among them, the tending of the enormous increment of school-age children.

At the other end of the age spectrum was the considerable growth in the elderly population (4.3 million people); in excess of 15 percent of the total national growth increment in the decade was 65 years of age and over. This increase in the elderly population provided impetus for the growth of a service and welfare-related job base for American society, which became more aware of the needs of the elderly. However, the sheer weight of youth more than offset the elderly expansion; this is reflected in the decline of the overall median age from 30.2 years to 29.4 years, gauging the beginning of the youth orientation that was to reach full force in the ensuing decade.

THE DECADE OF THE 1960s

The 1960s marked both the entrance of the early products of the baby boom into their college-age years and the advent of the baby bust. Indicating the latter was the abrupt decline (3.2 million) from 1960 to 1970 in the level of population under the age of five. This reflected in turn both the stagnancy and decline, respectively, of the proportion of the population in the prime childrearing ages of eighteen to twenty-four and twenty-five to thirty-four years during the previous decade, as well as the declining fertility rate of the 1960s.

At the same time, the five to seventeen years of age sector, the last remnants of the baby boom, continued to grow but at a diminished level from the 1950s,

EXHIBIT 6

ESTIMATED AGE STRUCTURE OF THE POPULATION OF THE UNITED STATES

JULY 1, 1950 TO JULY 1976[1]

(numbers in thousands)

Age (years)	1950	1950 to 1960 Change	1960	1960 to 1970 Change	1970	1970 to 1976 Change	1976
Total all ages	152,271	28,400	180,671	24,208	204,879	10,239	215,118
Under 5	16,410	3,931	20,341	-3,185	17,156	-1,817	15,339
5 to 17	30,878	13,306	44,184	8,362	52,546	-2,694	49,852
18 to 24	16,076	52	16,128	8,555	24,683	3,483	28,166
25 to 34	24,036	-1,117	22,919	2,374	25,293	6,751	32,044
35 to 44	21,637	2,584	24,221	-1,079	23,142	-66	23,076
45 to 54	17,453	3,125	20,578	2,732	23,310	332	23,642
55 to 64	13,396	2,229	15,625	3,039	18,664	1,400	20,064
65 and over	12,397	4,278	16,675	3,410	20,085	2,849	22,934
Median age	30.2		29.4		27.9		29.0

NOTE: 1. Includes Armed Forces overseas.

SOURCES: U.S. Bureau of the Census, *Current Population Reports*, Series P-25, No. 643, "Estimates of the Population of the United States, by Age, Sex, and Race:July 1, 1974 to 1976" (Washington, D.C.: U.S. Government Printing Office, January 1977); U.S. Bureau of the Census, *Statistical Abstract of the United States: 1976* (Washington, D.C.: U.S. Government Printing Office, 1976).

expanding by 8.4 million people. By 1970, this cohort accounted for over one quarter of the nation's population—52.5 million people—a level greater by 21.7 million people than that of 1950. America's school systems were severely stressed as their clientele peaked in number.

The largest variation, however, was in the eighteen to twenty-four years of age sector; in the 1950s, this cohort was extremely stable in size. In contrast, it expanded by 8.6 million people from 1960 to 1970, and with it the rapid expansion of the nation's educational infrastructure was transferred to the college and university scene. Concurrently, however, the problems of youth unemployment—and their sad corollary of juvenile delinquency—were clearly amplified.

The elderly continued to expand in absolute number, gaining 3.4 million people. The Sun Valleys and the retirement communities of Florida and New Jersey were bolstered by vigorous growth in their prime market targets. Nonetheless, the median age of Americans dropped to 27.9 years, as the "youth society" reached its apogee.

THE 1970 TO 1976 TRANSFORMATION

The contours of the baby bust continued to have an effect on American society in the decade of the 1970s, while the aging products of the baby boom dominated the total growth increment—two-thirds (6.8 million people) of the nation's 1970 to 1976 total growth (10.2 million people) were between the ages of twenty-five to thirty-four years, the period of household formation and peak childbearing. Similarly, the eighteen to twenty-four years of age cohort also continued to expand (3.5 million people) but at a lesser rate than that of the previous ten years.

Despite the burgeoning of these fertile sectors of society, the declining birth rates resulted in a 1.8 million person contraction in the under five years of age cohort. The decline of the latter during the preceding decade now had its impact on the five to seventeen years of age group which receded by 2.7 million people from 1970 to 1976. Excess capacity began to appear in the nation's school systems for the first time in the post-World War II era.

The rate of accession to the ranks of the elderly expanded markedly and, because of the declining number of births, the elderly comprised almost 28 percent of the national growth increment. As a result, the median age of Americans began to creep upward (29.0 years), as the era of an aging society began.

So by 1976 the outlines of the short term future have started to come into focus. The baby boom products are in their childbearing years, are forming households and are exerting pressures on the American economy to produce jobs for an unprecedented number of young adults. Similarly, the housing industry finds its major growth potential in the people of the twenty-five to thirty-four years of age cluster. To what type of housing does this group aspire? And what can they afford? These are questions of major import not only for the planning profession, but for America's political leadership as well. They should be kept in mind in reviewing the subsequent materials.

Contraction, also, is a phenomenon that will have to be grappled with. After three decades of struggling, often with indifferent results, in a milieu of growth, the wake of the baby boom is characterized by shrinking age cohorts. This in turn raises the problems of redundant infrastructures, excess capacities, and declining economic sectors. The educational professions are prime cases in point.

A myriad of other concerns are raised by this age structure transformation. It is important, therefore, to examine the short range projections under alternative assumptions.

THE IMMEDIATE FUTURE: 1976 TO 1985

The decline in the birth rate has been so precipitous as to leave demographers, both inside and out of the Census Bureau, gasping in its wake. Projection has followed projection, each one lower than its predecessor, yet still overly optimistic in terms of the realities of births that followed it. Indeed, the alternative projection sets presented in Exhibit 5 were issued in July, 1977 and supercede those published barely twenty months previously. For reasons that will be suggested subsequently—and for the purpose of economy and simplicity of presentation—only the Series II and III projections, which assume fertility rates moving toward the 2.1 and 1.7 levels, respectively, are employed in Exhibit 7.

In Exhibit 7, the results of these two alternatives, as well as the present base (1976), are detailed. It should be pointed out that for 1980 and 1985, the projections for the older groups are independent of the birth rate—the individuals are already alive and the total numbers of their respective age cohorts are reasonably assured, at least to the degree that the mortality rate and immigration assumptions are valid.

The maturing products of the baby boom continue to dominate the age structure changes—the bulk of the bulge will have aged to between twenty-five and thirty-four years of age by 1980. Indeed, the 4.1 million person increase in this cohort will account for between 59 percent and 74 percent of the national growth increment between 1976 to 1980.

Countering this expansion will be the sharp contraction by approximately 3 million people of the five to seventeen years of age cohort; the baby bust, then, will finally be affecting American society in full force. Between 1970 and 1980, it is entirely possible that the school age population will decline by over 6.6 million people, generating significant adjustments for educational and child-related institutions and services. Indeed, the school budget and school bond issues of yesteryear are giving way to the school-closing issues of today and tomorrow.

The prime executive cum technical and vocational age group, those people of thirty-five to forty-four years of age, will expand substantially, increasing by

EXHIBIT 7

ESTIMATED AND PROJECTED AGE STRUCTURE OF THE POPULATION OF THE UNITED STATES:
JULY 1, 1976 TO JULY 1, 1985
(numbers in thousands)

Age (years)	1976	Change 1976 to 1980		1980		Change 1980 to 1985		1985	
		Series II	Series III	Series II	Series III	Series II	Series III	Series II	Series III
Total all ages	215,118[1]	7,041	5,614	222,159	220,732	10,721	8,147	232,880	228,879
Under 5	15,339	681	-746	16,020	14,593	2,783	1,642	18,803	16,235
5 to 17	49,852	-3,892		45,960		-2,470	-3,903	43,490	42,057
18 to 24	28,166	1,296		29,462		-1,609		27,853	
25 to 34	32,044	4,128		36,172		3,687		39,859	
35 to 44	23,076	2,645		25,721		5,655		31,376	
45 to 54	23,642	-944		22,698		-241		22,457	
55 to 64	20,064	1,135		21,198		538		21,737	
65 and over	22,934	1,993		24,927		2,378		27,305	
Median Age	29.0			30.2	30.4			31.5	32.0

NOTE: 1. Includes Armed Forces overseas.

SOURCES: U.S. Bureau of the Census, *Current Population Reports*, Series P-25, No. 704, "Projections of the Population of the United States:1977 to 2050" (Washington, D.C.: U.S. Government Printing Office, July 1977); U.S. Bureau of the Census, *Current Population Reports*, Series P-25, No. 643, "Estimates of the Population of the United States, by Age, Sex, and Race:July 1, 1974 to 1976" (Washington, D.C.: U.S. Government Printing Office, January 1977).

more than 2.6 million people in the 1976 to 1980 period. While this will be offset partially by a decline of 1 million persons in the forty-five to fifty-four years of age group, clearly the competition for the executive suite will continue. Once again, the elderly are a significant growth sector with a net increase of 2 million people expected—or roughly 500,000 persons a year reaching the nominal retirement age and surviving between 1976 and 1980.

The enormous impact of relatively small changes in the fertility rate is shown in Exhibit 7 in the under five years of age group. If the nation were to return to the fertility rate of 1970–1971 (2.1), there would be a net addition of over 681,000 preschoolers. In contrast to this growth, the Series III projections, which embody current reality (a fertility rate of 1.7), show this cohort declining by 746,000, with concomitant implications through the history to come. But even a return of present fertility rate trends to those of earlier years would not preserve the United States population as a whole from a decided increase in median age to above thirty years.

THE EARLY 1980s

The overall aging of the population of the United States will continue to 1985, with the median age increasing beyond thirty-one years under both projection sets. By 1985, America's population will have grown by between 13.8 million and 17.7 million people from its 1976 base. The great baby boom bulge will have begun to enter the thirty-five to forty-four years of age sector, generating a 5.7 million person increase in this cohort. At the same time, the baby boom people will also dominate the twenty-five to thirty-four years of age sector, which will expand by 3.7 million people. The elderly will continue to escalate in number with a net addition of more than 2.3 million individuals over the age of sixty-five.

Regardless of whether it is the Series II or Series III projections that best mirror reality, there will be a continuation of the marked decline in the school-age population: a decrease of somewhere between 2.5 million and 3.9 million individuals. Equally significant, however, is the maturation of the baby bust cohort, which will clearly and specifically have an impact on the nation's institutions of higher learning. The number of people between the ages of eighteen and twenty-four years will decline by more than 1.6 million. A corollary to this impact will be a decline in the number of newcomers to the job market, a phenomenon on which attention will be focused subsequently.

When we contrast the age structure profile of America's population in 1976 with that of 1985, the scale of the transformation becomes evident. There will be a growth of more than 4.4 million people over the age of 65, plus a net addition of in excess of 1.6 million people between fifty-five and sixty-four years of age. The issues of retirement, pensions, social security, and social services to the elderly will become increasingly prominent and will place pressures concerning the need to support the elderly on an economic system already facing increasing international competition.

These problems may be accentuated by the decline (1.2 million) in the forty-five to fifty-four years of age cohort, the Depression era progeny, many of whom are in their peak earning years. Much of the immediate burden may rest on the twenty-five to thirty-four and the thirty-five to forty-four years of age groups (the baby boom products), whose numbers will increase by 7.8 million and 8.3 million people, respectively. It is paradoxical that a group born in perhaps the most affluent period in America's history, after facing a stagnant job market in the early 1970s and continual competition in the market place by virtue of its sheer numbers, should fall heir to the responsibility and burden of supporting an aging society.

In contrast, the eighteen to twenty-four years of age group will be in decline as the people born at the beginning of the baby bust reach adulthood. The main sag, however, will be experienced in the five to seventeen years of age cohort, which will have contracted by between 7.8 million and 6.4 million individuals. To say that these declines will challenge the conventions and assumptions established throughout the decade of the 1960s is to state the obvious. For example, turning to the more detailed age structure data, it is evident that there will be a decline of some 4 million persons in the thirteen to twenty-four years of age group between 1976 and 1985.[7] This cohort is the lifeblood of the soft-drink industry, with each individual consuming an average of 823 cans of soda each year.[8] Assuming this average consumption is valid for the next decade, 3.3 billion cans of soft drinks will *not* be sold in 1985 because of declines in this age group. Few industries and institutions will escape the impact of this demographic shift.

Finally the number of births will have inched upward regardless of which fertility assumption is employed, with the under five years of age group expanding by 896,000 under Series III and 3.5 million under Series II. The vital question of shifting fertility rates will be considered more fully in the summary of this chapter. First, however, the racial implications of the age structure evolution will be briefly reviewed.

RACIAL VARIATIONS

An increasing proportion of America's population, particularly in the younger age groups, is nonwhite. As shown in Exhibit 8, Negro and other races accounted for 12.4 percent of the total population in 1970; however, in the under five years of age cohort, they accounted for 15.7 percent. By 1975, the equivalent relationships were 13.1 percent and 17.3 percent, respectively.

By 1980, using the Census Bureau's Series II projections, their proportions will change to 13.8 percent and 17.1 percent, respectively. By 1985,

EXHIBIT 8
BLACK AND OTHER RACES AS A PERCENT OF TOTAL POPULATION,
SELECT AGE GROUPS: JULY 1, 1970 TO JULY 1, 1985[1]
(numbers in thousands)

Age (years)	1970	1975	1980 Series II	1985 Series II
Total all ages	12.4	13.1	13.8	14.4
Under 5	15.7	17.3	17.1	17.0
5 to 9	15.2	16.5	18.1	17.9
10 to 14	14.8	15.8	17.1	18.8
15 to 19	14.0	15.1	16.2	17.6
20 to 24	12.5	14.0	15.1	16.2
25 to 29	12.1	12.6	14.0	15.1

NOTE: 1. Includes Armed Forces overseas.

SOURCE: U.S. Bureau of the Census, *Current Population Reports,* Series P-25,
          No. 704, "Projections of the Population of the United States:1975 to 2050"
          (Washington, D.C.: U.S. Government Printing Office, July 1977).

nonwhites will comprise one out of seven of the total population as contrasted with one out of eight in 1970. Given their relatively youthful age skew, non-whites will make up nearly one in five of all children of grammar school age in 1985, and nearly that high a proportion of the population of fifteen to nineteen years of age. The implications of this growth have already been seen in the difficulties of developing school-busing programs to assure racial mix, particuarly in areas in which the number of whites—or their age distribution—is such as to limit the white student enrollment potential. And these difficulties will increase over time. But, given the total reduction in the number of newcomers in the age group entering the labor force, there will be both increased potential and challenge for American business to provide opportunity for blacks and other nonwhite groups. The job opportunities for minority youth, as the absolute number of whites in the equivalent age group is reduced, should expand. Americans, in general, and nonwhites in particular, have felt the stresses and limitations brought about by the enormous number of people in the age groups entering the labor force—but a time of unique opportunity may be very close at hand.

SUMMARY

The shifting patterns of childbearing in the three decades since World War II have had profound impact on the age structure of American society, and threaten the existence of a number of instrumentalities established in the past.

1. The youth society is gradually fading into the history text. Significant and sustained declines in the number of American citizenry between the ages of five and seventeen have been and will remain a fact of life.

2. Between 1970 and 1976, elementary school enrollment in the United States declined by 12.3 percent, or 4.2 million pupils.[9] Over the next decade, the balance of the nation's educational institutions will experience the same enrollment decline. School enrollments at all levels will have increasing proportions of nonwhites.

3. The ranks of the elderly are expanding. In 1976, over 10.6 percent of the population of America was sixty-five years of age and above, and this percentage will slowly increase in the future.

4. As a consequence of the above statistics, the nation's median age has started an upward climb—we are now experiencing the initial stages of what appears to be a long-term trendline. The aged-dependency ratio (the population over sixty-five years of age per 100 population aged eighteen to sixty-four years) is climbing upward. At the same time the child-dependency ratio (under eighteen years of age) has and will continue to decline.

5. If we are in the initial stages of an aging society, does this imply the advent of a more conservative milieu? Will there be greater resistance to change and new ideas? Will the no-growth and development-resisting forces dominate the day-to-day activities of the planning profession (at least where affluence has any influence)?

6. The dominant growth sector of present and future history will be the maturing cohorts of the baby boom. The population between the ages of twenty-five and forty-four years will be expanding markedly and will represent significant market targets. Yet, as a consequence of demography, this progeny of the 1946 to 1957 era will find competition, particularly in the job market, a constant part of life.

7. The present labor surplus—a result of the mass entrance of the baby boom products into the labor force—may well be transformed into a labor shortage over the decade of the 1980s as the shrinking cohorts of the subsequent baby bust reach adulthood. Will this result in improved job opportunities for minorities? Or will jobs be exported to foreign nations? Or, conversely, will illegal immigration continue and expand, perhaps under reclassification by modification of the nation's immigration statutes? And if the latter occurs, how will this immigration alter the age structure evolution.

8. Housing market shifts are at best always difficult to predict, and even more so on the basis of population alone. Indeed, the following chapters isolate patterns of household and employment trends and geographical movements that must be incorporated into any demand and supply equation. Still, the baby boom dynamic promises to dictate the demand for housing in the short-term future and, ignoring other factors, will exert pressure for single-family, suburban-type units.

9. A symptom of this demand was the multifamily construction surge throughout urban and suburban areas during the past decade. This can be construed, at least in part, as a lagged effect of the baby boom. As the instigators of this demand aged, the current single-family housing boom resulted. Yet household compositional changes lead one to question the longevity of this phenomenon.

4

Household Compositional Changes

Absolute population totals, even when disaggregated into detailed age cohorts, sketch but a partial picture of a very complex phenomenon. Of equal importance is the way individuals cluster into household configurations—groups of persons occupying individual housing units. Interpreted via this format, the implications of population change for the housing market, for example, become much more apparent. Indeed, housing demand is not so much a function of total population size, but rather of the total number of households. At the same time, however, the reality should not be overlooked that the very availability of housing may alter the scale of the household. In any case, as future land use requirements are defined, the realities of gross demographic variation must be viewed, at least in part, within the dynamics of household configurations. What are the realities and basic trends of this domain?

THE BROADER OUTLINES

In the period of one generation covered by Exhibit 9, there has been a remarkably consistent decline in the average household size in the United States. In the twenty-six years from 1950 to 1976, the average number of persons per household has dropped from 3.37 to 2.89, a decline of nearly 15 percent.[10] The implications of this shift can be emphasized by a simple illustration. Assume a political jurisdiction in 1950 having a base population of 1,000 people. By definition, if its average household size is 3.37 people, its housing units total 297. If by 1976 its absolute population size remains at the 1,000 level, 346 housing units are implied by an average household size of 2.89 people. Consequently, at the most basic level, areas of no-growth and stagnation may still experience surges of housing demand if the present household-size evolution persists into the future.

EXHIBIT 9
HOUSEHOLD-SIZE SHIFTS: 1950 TO 1976
(persons per household)

Year	Size
1950	3.37
1955	3.33
1960	3.33
1965	3.29
1970	3.14
1971	3.11
1972	3.06
1973	3.01
1974	2.97
1975	2.94
1976	2.89

SOURCE: U.S. Bureau of the Census, *Statistical Abstract of the United States:1976* (Washington, D.C.: U.S. Government Printing Office, 1976).

The household-size transformation to date is a composite of many elements and, as holds true for all of the concerns stressed here, the push-pull factors at work are of extreme complexity. Housing availability, income realities, welfare stipulations, and the enormous number of dynamics that are causally referred to as "changing societal and cultural norms" are all of significance. The analysis in this brief work must, of necessity, be limited to a very few of the principal parameters. It should be noted, however, that these are merely the external manifestations of enormously complex phenomena. The presentation, at best, must be limited to the topography rather than to the total dimensions of the realities embodied in the data.

A major attribute of the shrinking household size is the change in number of children born to individual women. This is reflected in Exhibit 10 which details the total children that were born per 1,000 married women and the percent childless for women ever married for the years 1960, 1970 and 1976. The importance of these changes in the number of children born is very clear: for all the age groups up to the age of thirty-nine years, there is a substantial decrease to the present time. (Those above forty years of age in 1976 were the principal generators of the baby boom detailed in the previous chapter). Unless there is an unparalleled increase of women having children in their later years, the future portends a continuation of the shrinking household-size trendline.

As shown in the second part of Exhibit 10, part of the pattern of decline is the result of the growing proportion of women under the age of thirty who are

EXHIBIT 10
CHILDREN EVER BORN PER 1,000
MARRIED WOMEN AND PERCENT
CHILDLESS FOR WOMEN EVER MARRIED:
1960 TO 1976[1]

Age (in years) of Women Ever Married	Children Ever Born Per 1,000 Married Women		
	1960	1970	1976
18 to 44	2,331	2,372	2,094
18 to 19	824	648	588
20 to 24	1,441	1,064	897
25 to 29	2,241	1,978	1,539
30 to 34	2,627	2,804	2,291
35 to 39	2,686	3,167	2,931
40 to 44	2,564	3,096	3,190
45 to 49	2,402	2,840	3,206

Age (in years) of Women Ever Married	Percent Childless for Women Ever Married		
	1960	1970	1976
15 to 44	15.0	16.4	18.8
15 to 19	43.6	50.7	55.1
20 to 24	24.2	35.9	41.7
25 to 29	12.6	15.8	21.7
30 to 34	10.4	8.3	10.5
35 to 39	11.1	7.4	6.6
40 to 44	14.1	8.6	7.5
45 to 49	18.1	10.8	7.8

NOTE: 1. Data are for resident population in 1960 and 1970 and for civilian noninstitutional population in 1976.

SOURCE: U.S. Bureau of the Census, *Current Population Reports,* Series P-20, No.
307, "Population Profile of the United States:1976" (Washington, D.C.: U.S.
Government Printing Office, April 1977).

married and have had no children. Again, this is a phenomenon mainly of the
women entering the childbearing years in the wake of the baby boom. But the
significant question concerns the extrapolation of these recent events into the
future. This crucial issue will be grappled with later in this chapter; first, the
events to date require further elaboration and analysis.

Changing household size is not solely a function of the rise and fall of the production of children; it is also accounted for by changes in the basic marriage relationship. As shown in Exhibit 11, the two major barometers, divorce and marriage rates, indicate changes that imply a decline in household size. Divorce rates over the last sixteen years, from 1960 to 1976, have increased by 127 percent, moving from 2.2 divorces per 1,000 population to the 5.0 level. The marriage rate has exhibited less drastic swings but, from 1972 to 1976, a downward trendline has been initiated, with the number of marriages per 1,000 population falling from 11.0 to 9.9. Indeed, there is some indication that the two indicators are converging. In 1950, the divorce rate was 23.4 percent of the marriage rate; by 1976, this relationship increased to 50.5 percent. While not every divorce necessarily ends in two separate households—with remarriage and other alternative living arrangements possible—it is a significant force in generating additional households.

Thus the broader outlines of a metamorphosis of the American household are apparent. A long-term decline in household size is manifest, resulting not only from declining fertility and fewer children, but from an increasing divorce rate and a declining marriage rate. Yet household size per se provides only a surface glimpse at a very complex evolution. What are the emerging household formats?

EXHIBIT 11
MARRIAGE AND DIVORCE RATES: 1950–1976

Year	Marriage Rate[1]	Divorce Rate[2]
1950	11.1	2.6
1955	9.3	2.3
1960	8.5	2.2
1965	9.3	2.5
1970	10.6	3.5
1971	10.6	3.7
1972	11.0	4.1
1973	10.9	4.4
1974	10.5	4.6
1975	10.0	4.8
1976	9.9	5.0

NOTES: 1. Number of marriages per 1,000 population.
2. Number of divorces per 1,000 population.
SOURCE: U.S. National Center for Health Statistics, *Vital Statistics of the United States*, annual.

EXHIBIT 12
HOUSEHOLDS BY TYPE AND SIZE: 1960 TO 1976[1]
(numbers in thousands)

Subject	1960		1970		1976		Percent Change	
	Number	Percent	Number	Percent	Number	Percent	1960–1970	1970–1976
Total Households	52,799	100.0	63,401	100.0	72,867	100.0	20.1	14.9
Primary Families	44,905	85.0	51,456	81.2	56,056	76.9	14.6	8.9
Husband-Wife	39,254	74.3	44,728	70.5	47,297	64.9	13.9	5.7
Male Head-No Wife Present	1,228	2.3	1,228	1.9	1,424	2.0	—	16.0
Female Head- No Husband Present	4,422	8.4	5,500	8.7	7,335	10.1	24.4	33.4
Primary Individuals	7,895	15.0	11,945	18.8	16,811	23.1	51.3	40.7
Living Alone[2]	6,896	13.1	10,851	17.1	14,983	20.6	57.4	38.1
With Nonrelative(s) Present	999	1.9	1,094	1.7	1,828	2.5	9.5	67.1
Average Size of Household	3.33		3.14		2.89			

NOTES: 1. As of March of the respective years. Noninstitutional population excluding Armed Forces in barracks.

2. One person households.

SOURCE: U.S. Bureau of the Census, *Current Population Reports*, Series P-20, No. 307, "Population Profile of the United States:1976" (Washington, D.C.: U.S. Government Printing Office, April 1977).

EMERGING HOUSEHOLD FORMATS

Exhibit 12 details the composition of America's households for 1960, 1970, and 1976. While the population growth (measured as of January 1—see Exhibit 1) from 1960 to 1970 was 13.6 percent, the growth in households was 20.1 percent. In the 1970 to 1976 period, the former expanded by 5.2 percent while the latter increased by 14.9 percent. Hence the gap between the two rates of growth is widening—and substantially.

As to the changing format of households, the most salient phenomenon is the decline in importance of primary husband-wife families. In 1960, they accounted for 74.3 percent of the nation's households. By 1976, their share had declined to 64.9 percent. At the same time, female-headed families (no husband present) increased from 8.4 percent of the total in 1960 to 10.1 percent in 1976. Overall, primary families (related family members sharing a dwelling unit), while not about to become extinct in America, have declined from 85.0 percent of the total households to 76.9 percent over this same period of time.

Households comprising primary individuals—either persons living alone or with nonrelatives only—increased quite rapidly and in 1976 accounted for 23.1 percent of all households, as compared to 15.0 percent in 1960. Indeed such nonfamily households increased more than four times as fast as family households from 1970 to 1976 (40.7 percent versus 8.9 percent). This increase in nonfamily households has resulted from substantial growth in single-person households—which had doubled in number to about the 15 million level by 1976—as well as from the emergence of a relatively new phenomenon: households comprising primary individuals and nonrelatives. In the six years from 1970 to 1976, this household type had the fastest growth rate of those shown here, increasing by 67.1 percent.

If we focus on the percentage changes for the latter period, the sharpness of the current trendlines—partially obscured in the former period by the longer time span—becomes evident. The number of households headed by primary individuals increased by 40.7 percent from 1970 to 1976 while primary families with female heads (no husband present) increased by 33.4 percent. Even male-headed primary families (no wife present) increased by 16.0 percent. At the same time, however, the husband and wife families expanded by only 5.7 percent. Consequently, what were once unique or atypical households are dominating the recent growth increment and require further analysis.

TWO PERSON HOUSEHOLDS

A significant portion of the primary individual households with non-relatives present comprise two person households (1.5 million out of 1.8 million such households in 1976). Exhibit 13 details their configuration by age of the household head for 1970 and 1976. The most significant increase occurred

EXHIBIT 13

TWO PERSON PRIMARY INDIVIDUAL HOUSEHOLDS BY AGE: 1970 to 1976[1]

(numbers in thousands)[2]

Age (in years) of Household Head (Primary Individual)	1970			1976		
	Primary Individ-uals in 2 Person Households	Sharing With Unrelated Person of Opposite Sex		Primary Individ-uals in 2 Person Households	Sharing With Unrelated Person of Opposite Sex	
		Number	Percent		Number	Percent
Total	991	327	33.0	1,479	660	44.6
Under 25	270	29	10.7	497	155	31.2
25 to 44	257	60	23.3	580	270	46.6
45 to 64	231	123	53.2	250	153	61.2
65 and over	234	115	49.1	152	83	54.6

NOTES: 1. Noninstitutional population excluding Armed Forces in barracks.
2. Numbers may not sum because of rounding.

SOURCE: U.S. Bureau of the Census, *Current Population Reports*, Series P-20, No. 307, "Population Profile of the United States:1976" (Washington, D.C.: U.S. Government Printing Office, April 1977).

in the number of primary individuals who shared their living quarters with an unrelated person of the opposite sex. Indeed, their number more than doubled, increasing from 327,000 in 1970 to 660,000 in 1976, and their percentage share of the total number of two-person households increased from 33.0 percent to 44.6 percent. While this phenomenon was mainly the province of older households in 1970, the critical mass, in terms of absolute numbers, has shifted to the younger age cohorts. But this is not merely a new fashion for America's young adults. The twenty-five to forty-four years of age category accounts for 40.9 percent (270,000) of the households of this genre, the largest single concentration.

While the rate of increase has been remarkable for the latter living arrangement, it should be emphasized that it accounts for only 3.9 percent of all primary individual households (660,000 out of 16.8 million), and is outnumbered by the single-person household by almost twenty-three to one (15.0 million to 660,000).

FEMALE FAMILY HEADS

Exhibit 14 presents the marital status of female family heads for 1960, 1970 and 1976. While the group as a whole increased 33.0 percent in the initial decade of this period, the increase was even larger, 34.1 percent, in the subsequent six years. Divorce on a proportionate basis has played a major role with an increment of 79.2 percent in the former period and 87.5 percent in the latter. Once again the contrast between the ten-year period and the subsequent six years should be noted. The second most striking increment was in the group of single women who, between 1970 and 1976, increased their numbers by 59.8 percent.

Some of these shifts may well be more step functions than dynamic in nature, such as those changes in divorce status occasioned by the rise of simplified no-fault approaches within local law. Similarly, new opportunities for women may make single status as head of household more economically feasible.

Regardless of the forces at work, however, they are unequally shared when they are analyzed by racial characteristics as shown at the bottom of Exhibit 14. The 1970 to 1976 growth rate of white female family heads was 28.6 percent and the equivalent for black female family heads was 48.6 percent. While the two diverse proportions show some signs of narrowing—the former increased from its 1960 to 1970 rate while the latter declined—to the degree that female-headed households tend to have relatively low incomes—if not poverty status—their increase in numbers is most ominous for social planners. Much of the absolute growth is the residual of broken families; some of it, however, represents the increased proportion of women who have never married.

EXHIBIT 14

MARITAL STATUS OF FEMALE FAMILY HEADS: 1960 TO 1976[1]

(numbers in thousands)

	1960	1970	1976	Percent Change 1960–1970	1970–1976
All Female Family Heads	4,196	5,580	7,482	33.0	34.1
Single	487	610	975	25.3	59.8
Married, Spouse Absent	914	1,324	1,772	44.9	33.8
Widowed	2,093	2,389	2,376	14.1	-0.5
Divorced	702	1,258	2,359	79.2	87.5
White Female Family Heads	3,306	4,185	5,380	26.6	28.6
Black Female Family Heads	890	1,349	2,004	51.6	48.6

NOTE: 1. Noninstitutional population excluding Armed Forces in barracks.

SOURCE: U.S. Bureau of the Census, *Current Population Reports,* Series P-20. No. 307, "Population Profile of the United States:1976" (Washington, D.C.: U.S. Government Printing Office, April 1977).

SINGLE (NEVER MARRIED) WOMEN

Irrespective of their household and family membership status, the proportion of women remaining single is experiencing a demonstrable upswing. As shown in Exhibit 15, this trend is particularly characteristic of the more youthful women of our society. The proportion of women twenty to twenty-four years of age who had never married in 1976 (42.6 percent) was half again as high as the equivalent for 1960 (28.4 percent), with a similar evolution over time in the twenty-five to twenty-nine years of age category. The increase in the twenty to twenty-four year old cohort is particularly significant since this is the age when most women traditionally have married. Moreover, in conjunction with the increased prevalence of nonmarriage in the subsequent age group (twenty-five to twenty-nine years), it may suggest the general acceptance by young women of either postponing marriage or remaining single throughout their entire lives.

It is interesting to note the reverse pattern as we focus on the older age groups. In 1960 there was a far higher proportion of women, particularly in

EXHIBIT 15
PERCENT SINGLE (NEVER MARRIED) WOMEN
BY AGE: 1960 TO 1976[1]

Age (in years)	1960	1970	1976
Total, 14 and over	19.0	22.1	23.0
Under 35	37.6	44.4	45.3
Over 35	7.2	6.1	5.0
20 to 24	28.4	35.8	42.6
25 to 29	10.5	10.5	14.8
30 to 34	6.9	6.2	7.0
35 to 39	6.1	5.4	5.2
40 to 44	6.1	4.9	4.2
45 to 54	7.0	4.9	4.4
55 to 64	8.0	6.8	4.9
65 and over	8.5	7.7	5.9

NOTE: 1. Noninstitutional population excluding Armed Forces in barracks.

SOURCE: U.S. Bureau of the Census, *Current Population Reports,* Series P-20, No.
307, "Population Profile of the United States:1976" (Washington, D.C.: U.S.
Government Printing Office, April 1977).

those age categories above forty-five years, who had never been married than
holds true currently. Is this pattern the residual of trends earlier in this century
in Suffragettism? Is it related in part, particularly among the middle-aged
members of this group, to the Depression years? Or does it perhaps indicate
that in the future we will see a shift toward later marriage? And if it is the last,
what impact will that have on population growth? Some light may be focused on
this question by examining the birth expectations of wives.

BIRTH EXPECTATIONS OF WIVES

Exhibit 16 presents the birth expectations of wives according to age and
race from 1967 to 1976. The data are based upon survey questions regarding
how many births women of various age categories anticipate. In general, in
every period it is the more youthful wives who have the lowest birth expectations. The shrinkage is substantial; in 1967 while wives aged between eighteen
and twenty-four years anticipated 2.85 births, their peers in the thirty-five to
thirty-nine year range were expecting approximately 3.3 births. Moreover the

EXHIBIT 16
BIRTH EXPECTATIONS OF WIVES BY AGE AND RACE
1967 (FEBRUARY-MARCH) TO 1976 (JUNE)
(births expected per 1,000 wives)

	Births expected by wives aged—			
	18–24 Years	25–29 Years	30–34 Years	35–39 Years
Total				
1967	2,852	3,037	3,288	3,299
1975 (June)	2,172	2,260	2,610	3,058
1976	2,141	2,202	2,535	2,994
White				
1967	2,859	3,001	3,200	3,215
1975 (June)	2,147	2,233	2,564	2,989
1976	2,127	2,175	2,514	2,949
Black				
1967	2,787	3,407	4,257	4,226
1975 (June)	2,481	2,583	3,213	3,957
1976	2,304	2,508	2,923	3,579

SOURCE: U.S. Bureau of the Census, *Current Population Reports,* Series P-20, No. 307, "Population Profile of the United States:1976," (Washington, D.C.: U.S. Government Printing Office, April 1977).

decline over time for equivalent age groups is pervasive. Again the most youthful category (those eighteen to twenty-four years of age) in 1976 anticipated a rate of only 2.141, a close approximation of zero population growth. Their older peers in the twenty-five to twenty-nine years of age cohort were at the 2.202 level, while the oldest category shown here, thirty-five to thirty-nine years of age, expected 2.994 children.

The basic patterns continue when the data are partitioned by race. While birth expectations of blacks are somewhat higher, particularly for the older age groups, they are strikingly comparable to those of the white group for the eighteen to twenty-four years of age category (2.127 versus 2.304). To the degree that these expectations are appropriate forecasts for the future, even if marriage (for the moment assumed as a preliminary to births) takes place at a later life stage, the resulting number of children will be relatively modest. And, certainly, these data are enhanced if we consider responses of all women, including those who are not currently married, as shown in Exhibit 17. The "all women" category by age group in general has lower expected lifetime births than has the "currently married" category. The "widowed, divorced, and separated" category also has lower expected lifetime births (with the exception of the thirty to thirty-four years of age cohort—and the response of this age group may well be based to a large degree on past experience). Certainly, then, there is no indication in the response of the singles group that there is a potential reservoir of additional births to be anticipated from its ranks.

ARE TRENDS DESTINY?

One of the few definitive propositions that have emerged from social science research would deny any sweeping affirmative response to the rhetorical question posed in this subtitle. It is equally evident, however, that long-term phenomena of substantial sweep must receive considerable respect as we attempt to view the future. In this context, the long-term birth-rate evolution (the number of live births per 1,000 total population) from 1820 to 1976 deserves careful study (see Exhibit 18). The first 100 years of the period saw a steady decline, from the 55.2 level of 1820 to half of that (27.7) in 1920. The 1940 rate of 19.4 represents an acceleration in the decline compared to the gradual lessening of the earlier periods, a reflection of the extraordinary circumstances of the Depression. What is more significant, however, is the explosion of the birth rate in 1947 (to the 26.6 level) and the resumption of the long-term pattern of decline after that date. It is indeed possible to view the immediate post-World War II baby boom as a short-term aberration compensating for Depression era deficits without necessarily invalidating the century-long secular trendline.

In the context of the recent acceleration of decline in the birth rate (38 percent in sixteen years), and the long-term dynamic, what should we expect in the future?[11] Certainly, the sharp downturn of the decade of 1930s and the compensating upsurge in 1947 could provide the logic for predicting an analogous self-corrective measure to occur in the short-term future. What such a scenario could imply would be a temporary upswing to the long-term trendline and then the subsequent resumption of slow but continuously declining birth rates.

What proves faulty in this analogy, however, concerns the severity of the economic and social dislocations—the Depression and World War II—that underlay the distorted birth rates of 1940 and 1947. While our own era has its share of traumas, it is difficult to match their disruptive influences to that of those earlier events. And, even they, despite their severity, were but temporary in terms of the long sweep of history.

We would hazard the assertion that there are no equivalent traumas underlying recent events, and that any sharp deviation is unlikely in their absence. To cause a significant shift in the social and cultural forces that affect the birth rate will probably require threshold changes on the order of those

EXHIBIT 17

BIRTHS TO DATE AND LIFETIME BIRTHS EXPECTED PER 1,000 WOMEN BY MARITAL STATUS: JUNE 1976

Age Group (in years)	All Women		Currently Married (Except Separated)		Widowed, Divorced, and Separated		Single	
	Births to Date	Lifetime Births Expected	Births to Date	Lifetime Births Expected	Births to Date	Lifetime Births Expected	Births to Date	Lifetime Births Expected
18 to 24	528	2,031	818	2,141	1,136	1,942	161	1,931
25 to 29	1,442	2,099	1,569	2,202	1,725	2,161	424	1,424
30 to 34	2,266	2,445	2,362	2,535	2,458	2,575	535	939
35 to 44	N.A.	N.A.	2,994	2,994	N.A.	N.A.	N.A.	N.A.

NOTE: N.A. = not available.

SOURCE: U.S. Bureau of the Census, *Current Population Reports*, Series P-20, No. 307, "Population Profile of the United States:1976" (Washington, D.C.: U.S. Government Printing Office, April 1977).

EXHIBIT 18
THE SECULAR TRENDLINE:
TOTAL BIRTH RATE: 1820–1976[1]

Year	Rate
1820	55.2
1840	51.8
1860	44.3
1880	39.8
1900	32.3
1920	27.7
1940	19.4
1947	26.6
1960	23.7
1970	18.4
1976	14.7

NOTE: 1. Number of live births per 1,000 total population.
SOURCE: U.S. National Center for Health Statistics, *Vital Statistics of the United States* annual.

prevalent from 1930 to 1945. Also, the forces presently in motion—the maturation of the women's movement, contraception, and abortion, for example—appear not to be temporary, but on the verge of permanent institutionalization. The labor and workforce parameters of the following section also provide some evidence of this assumption.

Consequently, the extrapolation of the long-term secular trendline—of gradual and perhaps decreasing declines—stands as our expectation for the short-term future. However, slight but temporary upward fluctuations remain a distinct possibility, which, because of the large number of women of childbearing age, could cause the resulting output to be considerable in magnitude.

There is perhaps one certainty in our hesitant prognostications—their validity can be evaluated very quickly. The initial and oldest products of the baby boom are now reaching thirty years of age. Since it is desirable for women to have children before the age of thirty-five, the birth rate of the next several years will be a key lead indicator of the future. If there is no significant increase by the early 1980s, the probability of the continuation of the present trendline will be very high.[12]

SUMMARY

The American household is undergoing a basic transformation as the currents of social change assume new directions. The following is a summary of the more pertinent parameters attendant to these phenomena:

1. The most visible manifestation of the evolving household of America is its reduction in scale. Between 1950 and 1976, it declined slowly but consistently from an average size of 3.37 persons to 2.89 persons.
   a. A key input into this contraction is the declining fertility rate specified earlier, and the increasing rate of childlessness among young married women.
   b. Another major factor comprises fundamental changes in the marriage relationship. The divorce rate has more than doubled over the past fifteen years, while the marriage rate has declined in the last five. There is some indication that a general pattern of postponing marriage is an increasingly prevalent norm for young women.

2. Subsumed under the cloak of the household size transformation are the changing formats of the nation's households. The traditional husband and wife module by itself is no longer a sufficient descriptor. A new typology has to be formulated.
   a. Primary husband-wife families accounted for three-quarters of America's households in 1960; by 1976, their share declined to below two-thirds. In the 1970 to 1976 period, they were the slowest growing household type (5.7 percent).
   b. In contrast, female family heads increased by one-third (33.4 percent) after 1970. Families headed by women with no husband present, then, represent a growing proportion of America's households. For the most part, this change has resulted from the increasing divorce rate.
   c. Nonfamily households (primary individuals) have experienced a remarkable growth surge over the past sixteen years, accounting for 23.1 percent of all households in 1976 (compared to 15.0 percent in 1960). In 1976, 89 percent of nonfamily households comprised a single person.
   d. The other nonfamily category, primary individuals sharing a dwelling unit with nonrelatives, was the fastest growing household type, increasing by 67.1 percent between 1970 and 1976.
   e. And subsumed within the latter format are unrelated adults of the opposite sex sharing two-person households. Although their absolute number is small (660,000 in 1976), they represent the fastest expanding living arrangement in the nation with their ranks more than doubling in the past six years.

3. The institutionalization of these new conventions is gauged by declining birth expectations, particularly among the younger age cohorts, not only of married women, but of single, widowed, divorced, and separated women.

4. In an era of ever increasing housing costs, do the new formats of the American household (particularly as they imply a diminished importance for child-oriented families) portend the emergence of a new base upon which to hinge the revitalization of America's troubled central cities? Can the first generation born and reared in the nation's suburbs be lured to the central cities where its parents were born and raised? Will the cities be able to marshall their resources to meet the challenge of the ostensible opportunities?

5. Despite the heroic efforts of the past, it is difficult to refute the lack of success in deflecting the downward trends of the urban centers of America. Yet, the age-structure shifts of the twenty-five years following World War II virtually dictated the emergence of mass suburbia, overwhelming most central city initiatives. With the age-structure and household patterns now assuming new formats, at least part of the rationale for suburbia is removed. Is the time at hand when efforts at revitalizing central cities will be congruent to the social trendlines? It will indeed be paradoxical if a resurgence of urban living occurs spontaneously (i.e. without significant governmental effort) just as the national commitment to cities has virtually disintegrated.

6. This leads to the question of broad housing demand. While age structure shifts imply a single-family boom, the household transformation may dampen this possibility, at least if the soaring housing-cost variable is entered into the equation. One important factor in this context is the desire for single-family units by smaller households, even if they lack children. There are sporadic indications that this may well be the rule rather than the exception.

7. Despite, or perhaps in consequence of, soaring housing costs, the single-family unit is the major inflationary-proof vehicle available to most Americans. If housing is viewed not strictly in terms of shelter functions but in reference to investment and capital accumulation criteria, then the rationale for single-family units remains, whatever contractions occur in the child-rearing pressures. Yet, before definitive conclusions can be risked, labor force and employment variables must be reviewed.

5

Population and Labor Force
Growth Patterns

Changes in fertility rates, their reflection in diminished population growth and shifting age structures, and their interrelationship with evolving household configurations probably cannot occur without corresponding changes in the patterns of labor force participation. Yet, it is probably impossible to suggest which variable is causal. Do lower fertility rates enable more women to enter the labor force, thereby attaining the means to establish separate households? Or do increased consumption requirements necessitate women entering the labor force, thereby causing reduced fertility rates?'To view the problem in terms of discrete linear causal relationships is futile. America's changing population landscape is the product of a number of factors interacting with and reinforcing one another, eventually coalescing into a dynamic whose surface at best is described by the data available.

Consequently, a corollary to the changes already described are the emerging labor force and employment patterns of individuals and households. The former will be the focus of the immediate discussion, while the latter will be reserved for the following chapter.

The realities of growth in GNP (Gross National Product), of unemployment and of many aspects of social service delivery requirements are strongly influenced by changes in the scale and composition of the labor force by itself. As we shall note later, changes in the labor force, though linked to variations in the size of the population of working age, are far from directly determined by it. The shifts in participation rates of people of both sexes in specific age groups may be more consequential than the absolute growth of the particular age cohorts.[13]

POPULATION AND LABOR FORCE

Exhibit 19 presents the growth of the noninstitutional working-age population (sixteen years of age and over) and the civilian labor force from 1950 to

EXHIBIT 19
POPULATION AND LABOR FORCE:
1950 TO 1976
(numbers in thousands)

Year	Total Noninstitutional Population[1]	Civilian Labor Force		
		Total	Male	Female
1950	106,645	62,208	43,819	18,389
1955	112,721	65,023	44,475	20,548
1960	119,759	69,628	46,388	23,240
1965	129,236	74,455	48,255	26,200
1970	140,182	82,715	51,195	31,520
1976	156,048	94,773	56,259	38,414
	Percent Increase			
1950–1976	46.3	52.3	28.6	108.9

NOTE: 1. 16 years of age and over.

SOURCES: U.S., Department of Labor, Bureau of Labor Statistics, *Employment and Earnings: March 1977* Vol. 24, No. 3 (Washington, D.C.: U.S. Government Printing Office, 1977); U.S., Department of Labor and the U.S., Department of Health, Education, and Welfare, *Employment and Training Report of the President* (Washington, D.C.: U.S. Government Printing Office, 1977).

1976. Over the long term (1950 to 1976), while population increased by 46.3 percent, the labor force increased by 52.3 percent. Indeed, if the labor force participation rate was the same in 1976 as in 1950 (58.3 percent), there would be 91 million people in the labor force instead of the actual total of 94.8 million.

As is evident, the differential is the product of the increased participation in the labor force of American women. Their ranks swelled by 108.9 percent over the twenty-six year period, over twice as fast as the population increase and almost four times as fast as the growth of males (28.6 percent) in the labor force.

The impetus for this phenomenon takes many forms—the women's movement, the changing pattern of occupations in a postindustrial society (whereby many of today's jobs can be handled by either sex), the introduction of labor-saving devices and conveniences in the home (providing emancipation from historical housewife functions) and changing cost-of-living parameters (or consumption requirements and desires). Whatever interacting causal

EXHIBIT 20
WOMEN IN THE LABOR FORCE[1]
(numbers in thousands)

Year	Female Population[1] 16 Years and Over	Those in Civilian Labor Force	Percent in Labor Force
1950	54,293	18,389	33.9
1955	57,610	20,548	35.7
1960	61,615	23,240	37.7
1965	66,763	26,200	39.2
1970	72,774	31,520	43.3
1976	81,309	38,414	47.2
Percent Increase			
1950–1976	49.8	108.9	—
1970–1976	11.7	21.9	—

NOTE: 1. Noninstitutional population.

SOURCES: U.S., Department of Labor, Bureau of Labor Statistics, *Employment and Earnings: March, 1977* Vol. 24, No. 3 (Washington, D.C.: U.S. Government Printing Office, 1977); U.S., Department of Labor and the U.S., Department of Health, Education, and Welfare, *Employment and Training Report of the President* (Washington, D.C.: U.S. Government Printing Office, 1977).

forces are operative, it is clear that the phenomenon represents, not a temporary surge, but a long term reality.

WOMEN IN THE LABOR FORCE

The vigorous advance of female participation in the labor force is detailed in Exhibit 20. In 1950, approximately one-third (33.9 percent) of the female population sixteen years of age and over were in the civilian labor force. By 1976, it was nearly one out of two (47.2 percent), despite the increasing diversion of the female population into forms of higher education, and the comparatively small number of working women sixty-five years of age and over.

The pattern of growth in the participation of females in the labor force is not limited to younger women—it is pervasive across all age categories. Exhibit 21 details the transformation between 1947 and 1977. In the former year, the pattern is one of heavy participation in the twenty to twenty-four year old category (45 percent), a diminution in the earlier years of childbearing

EXHIBIT 21
SELECT AGE GROUP CHARACTERISTICS—
LABOR FORCE PARTICIPATION RATES:
1947 TO FEBRUARY 1977[1]

Age Group (in years)	Females in Labor Force (Rate)	
	1947	1977 (February)
20 to 24	44.9%	65.0%
25 to 34	32.0	49.0
35 to 44	36.3	59.2
45 to 54	32.7	55.4
55 to 64	24.3	41.3
65 and over	8.1	8.3
	Males in Labor Force (Rate)	
	1947	1977 (February)
45 to 54	95.5%	91.1%
55 to 64	89.6	74.0
65 and over	47.8	19.7

NOTE: 1. Total labor force.

SOURCES: U.S., Department of Labor, Bureau of Labor Statistics, *Employment and Earnings: March 1977* Vol. 24, No. 3 (Washington, D.C.: U.S. Government Printing Office, 1977); U.S., Department of Labor and the U.S., Department of Health, Education, and Welfare, *Employment and Training Report of the President* (Washington, D.C.: U.S. Government Printing Office, 1977).

(twenty-five to thirty-four years) to the 32 percent level, a slight increase for the thirty-five to forty-four years of age category (36 percent), with declines evident for subsequent cohorts. The 1976 pattern shows a substantial growth enhancement for every age classification. Indeed, at the twenty to twenty-four years of age level, nearly two out of three women (65 percent) are in the labor force. However, the prevalance of higher education opportunities have probably acted as a retardant to even more dramatic growth. Consequently, the largest changes over time are in the province of older women.

To the degree that these changes are a function of shifts in occupation to those that are performed equally well by either sex (with paper work, for example, replacing physical labor), male workers face increasing competition. Perhaps one of its manifestations lies in the fact that many men are dropping out of the labor force into early retirement. As shown at the bottom of

Exhibit 21, the labor force participation rate of older males has declined sharply over the past thirty years. Indeed, in 1947, almost half (47.8 percent) of the nation's males sixty-five years of age and over were still in the labor force. Presently (1977), only one-fifth (19.7 percent) are still active participants. Equally significant, although smaller in magnitude, is the participation rate decline for men fifty-five to sixty-four years of age. To what extent, then, are the female inroads linked to the male demise? While we are unable to answer this question, the fact that over half (52.8 percent) of the females of working age are not in the labor force (perhaps representing an untapped pool for increase) makes the answer of vital concern for future public policy, particularly since the nation is now experiencing rapid growth in the twenty-five to forty-four years of age population, detailed earlier in the age-structure discussion.

SUMMARY

The evolution of the United States into a postindustrial economy in the past quarter century has been accompanied by dramatic increases in the size of the labor force. The mythology of a leisure society is giving way to the reality of a two-sex nonfamily work society.

1. While the working-age population of America increased by 46.3 percent from 1950 to 1976, the labor force increased by 52.3 percent.

2. This differential emerged despite the sharp declines in the labor force participation rates of men over the age of sixty-five, since early retirement has become increasingly common. Indeed, the male component of the labor force did not keep pace with population growth, increasing by only 28.6 percent from 1950 to 1976.

3. In contrast, the rapid expansion of the female labor force (108.9 percent over the past twenty-six years) appears as one of the more striking trendlines of recent history. The labor force participation rate of women increased from 33.9 percent in 1950 to 47.2 percent in 1976.

The implications of this phenomenon by itself are myriad, not the least of which is reflected in the substantial increase in unemployment throughout the 1970s. Moreover, given the changing age structure of America and the rapid accession of the baby boom residuals into the labor force—as well as the unknown dimension of illegal immigration—the American economy may be severely strained to provide full employment in the very short-term future. Moreover, the competition presently facing our minority-group citizenry in this context cannot be minimized. But other repercussions are amplified as they manifest themselves within the family unit.

6

Family and Employment Characteristics

The mutually reinforcing characteristics of social events, the push versus the pull factors and their coalescence, defy casual analysis. When we turn to the tremendous changes that have taken place in the employment characteristics of husband and wife households, certainly this dilemma becomes evident. How do we quantify the role of inflation in making the burden of maintaining a standard of living so onerous as to require multiple wage earners, of the current escalation in housing costs in encouraging both husband and wife to participate in the labor force, of the feminine awareness, of a new consciousness of the necessity to have independent economic incomes as marriage becomes more transient? These, and a host of other factors, obviously play a role in the dynamics underlying the data presented in this chapter. Regardless of the causal elements, the results are at hand and their influence is of enormous import in the present and future patterns of development within the United States.

SPOUSES WORKING AND IN THE LABOR FORCE

The events documented in the previous chapter cannot be attributed to the soaring divorce rates and the declining marriage rates detailed earlier. The pattern of working women is even more exaggerated as husband-wife families are examined. Exhibit 22 indicates that the number of employed husbands in husband-wife families increased by 23 percent for the twenty-nine years from April 1947 to March 1976. In the equivalent period, the number of employed wives increased by 208 percent, nearly ten times as fast. Indeed, despite the relatively low base level for the latter group, the absolute increment in the number of employed wives (13.5 million) was nearly double the increment in the number of employed husbands.

There were two factors at hand that account for the arithmetic—if not the

EXHIBIT 22
WORKING SPOUSES: 1947 TO 1976[1]
(numbers in thousands)

Date	Employed Husbands	Employed Wives
April 1947	29,865	6,502
March 1976	36,735	20,023
1947–1976 Percent Change	23.0	208.0

NOTE: 1. Husband or wife employed, spouse present; sixteen years of age and over beginning 1967; fourteen years of age and over until 1967.

SOURCE: U.S., Department of Labor and U.S., Department of Health, Education, and Welfare, *Employment and Training Report of the President* (Washington, D.C.: U.S. Government Printing Office, 1977).

phenomena: the first of these was a decline in labor force participation rates of husbands. As shown in Exhibit 23, they declined from 91.6 percent in 1950 to 82.1 percent in 1976. And the second factor was that, at the same time, the labor force participation rate of wives virtually doubled, from the 23.8 percent level in the base year to 45.0 percent in 1976. Given the typical American pattern of husbands being older than wives, this may in part reflect the pattern of earlier retirement for the men. But, nevertheless, the reality of a basic transformation is certainly obvious.

MULTIPLE WORKER FAMILIES

It should be noted in this context that the proportion of families with two workers or more does not necessarily mean that one of those workers will be a wife. As shown in Exhibit 24, some 36.1 percent of husband-wife families had two workers or more in 1950, with the labor force participation rate of wives only 23.8 percent. By 1975, the equivalent proportions were 48.7 and 44.4 percent, respectively. While this does not necessarily imply a labor force participation rate reduction for nonhusbands or nonwives within the household, there are indications from the previous exhibits that such individuals are decreasingly present. The formation of separate households at an earlier age by the younger generation has been influential. Again, the causal linkage is obscure. As the younger generation exits, does the wife have to work to main-

EXHIBIT 23
Spouse in Labor Force: 1950 to 1976[1]
(Labor Force Participation Rates)[2]

Year	Husband	Wives
1950	91.6	23.8
1955	90.7	27.7
1960	88.9	30.5
1965	87.7	34.7
1970	86.9	40.8
1975	82.8	44.4
1976	82.1	45.0

NOTES: 1. Husbands or wife in labor force, spouse present.
2. Rates are for March of each year, except for 1955, which is for April.

SOURCE: U.S., Department of Labor and U.S., Department of Health, Education, and Welfare, *Employment and Training Report of the President* (Washington, D.C.: U.S. Government Printing Office, 1977).

tain the rent-paying capacity of the family? Or has the shift out of the household by the younger generation been made feasible by the wife/mother working? Interpenetrating these questions is the inclusion of elderly workers, perhaps of an older generation, within the family unit. The older worker in the younger family unit may have been much more common in 1950 than today, when the elderly maintain separate households in retirement enclaves.

Again the push-pull inputs are all too complex. Does the financial capacity achieved by the wife working lead to the dissolution of the extended family unit, or are the dynamics behind the latter even broader—suggesting both the necessity and the relative freedom of the wife participating in the labor force? Obviously neither of these precludes the other—the respective shares, however, remain obscure.

Regardless of the elements at work here, the present composition (1975) of husband-wife families from a labor force participation point of view is shown in Exhibit 25. The single largest category has both principals in the labor force (41 percent). Significantly, in only one-third (34 percent) of America's husband-wife families is the husband the sole participant in the labor force. Moreover, 12 percent of the families have no one in the labor force—typically, the retired, though there are other phenomena subsumed in this group. The other configurations are small in number.

Put at its simplest, then, more than four in ten of all "whole" households

EXHIBIT 24
TRENDS IN THE PROPORTION OF HUSBAND-WIFE FAMILIES
WITH TWO WORKERS OR MORE AND THE LABOR FORCE PARTICIPATION
RATES OF WIVES: MARCH 1950 TO MARCH 1975

Year[1]	Proportion of Families with Two Workers or More	Labor Force Participation Rate of Wives
1950	36.1	23.8
1955	36.2	27.7
1960	38.3	30.5
1965	41.6	34.7
1970	46.2	40.8
1975	48.7	44.4

NOTE: 1. March to March except for 1955, which is April.

SOURCE: Howard Hayghe, "Families and the Rise of Working Wives—An Overview,"
          Monthly Labor Review (May 1976):13.

are ones in which both husband and wife are actively participating in the labor
force. In only one out of three cases is the husband solely in the labor force;
and in one out of eight cases, no one is in the labor force. The new family pattern of the United States, if we can reverse this data, is one in which the earlier
classic module, of the husband working outside the household with the wife
substantially confined within it, is in the minority.

This new pattern of life extends even to married women with school-age
children. As shown in Exhibit 26, the labor force participation rate of married
women with such children has risen from 28.3 percent in 1950 to 53.7 percent in
1976. Indeed, it is most striking to note that this rate is substantially higher
than for wives in total, reflecting the higher labor participation rate of relatively
youthful women—those who have children between the ages of five and seventeen. It also indicates, however, the decline in the classic role of childrearer
which historically devolved—though never completely—upon married women.
It is relevant also that this shift has taken place without major technological or
organizational adjustments (outside the home) with which to buffer the
change. Indeed, the latter have tended to lag behind the basic shift. Only
recently, for example, has industry begun to adapt to the potential economies
of part-time labor. Within the household, however, the complement to the labor
force participation rate of women is more clearly seen in the additional number
of mechanized and electronic household aids.

EXHIBIT 25
HUSBAND-WIFE FAMILIES BY LABOR FORCE
STATUS OF FAMILY MEMBERS: MARCH, 1975

	Percent of Total
Husband and Wife in Labor Force	41
Husband Only in Labor Force	34
None in Labor Force	12
Husband and Other in Labor Force	8
Wife Only in Labor Force	3
More than One Family Member in Labor Force, Excluding Husband	1
Other Family Member Only in Labor Force	1
TOTAL	100

SOURCE: Howard Hayghe, "Families and the Rise of Working Wives—An Overview," *Monthly Labor Review* (May 1976):16.

THE INCOME DIMENSION

The results of the shifts in work and labor-force patterns within the family are mirrored by the evolving variation between the average weekly earnings for individual workers versus median family incomes (see Exhibit 27). While the former grew by 209.4 percent between 1950 and 1975, the latter increased half as much again—by 313.3 percent over the same time period. And this in turn is further reflected by the growing variation in median family income as a function of the wife in the labor force. As shown in Exhibit 28, by 1974 the median family income for families with wives in the labor force was close to $17,000 while, if the wife was not in the labor force, the median income dropped to the $12,000 level. Much of the new consumer affluence of the American household is a tribute to the distaff monetary input.

But note that this dollar gap may be much exaggerated. It does not take into account, for example, the unpaid services typically provided by the "at home" wife that to a certain extent must now be contracted out and/or purchased. The stagnancy of the supermarket industry in the face of the burgeoning fast-food chains stands as a prototypical symptom. Furthermore the gross data do not show the influence of federal income tax and social security policy—as well as the expenses that tend to parallel the work-associated

EXHIBIT 26
MARRIED WOMEN (HUSBAND PRESENT) IN THE LABOR FORCE,
WITH SCHOOL-AGE CHILDREN[1]

Year	Labor Force Participation Rate[2]
1950	28.3
1955	34.7
1960	39.0
1965	42.7
1970	49.2
1975	52.4
1976	53.7

NOTES: 1. Children six to seventeen years of age.
         2. As of March of the respective years.

SOURCE: U.S. Bureau of the Census, *Statistical Abstract of the United States:1976*
         (Washington, D.C.: U.S. Government Printing Office, 1976).

EXHIBIT 27
WEEKLY PAY VS. FAMILY INCOME

Year	Average Weekly Earnings[1]	Median Family Income
1950	$53	$3,319
1955	68	4,421
1960	81	5,620
1965	95	6,957
1970	119	9,867
1975	164	13,719
	Percent Increase	
1950 to 1975	209.4	313.3

NOTE: 1. Gross averages, production or nonsupervisory workers on private non-
         agricultural payrolls.

SOURCES: U.S. Department of Labor, Bureau of Labor Statistics *Monthly Labor
         Review,* monthly; U.S. Bureau of the Census, *Current Population Reports,*
         Series P-20, No. 307, "Population Profile of the United States:1976" (Wash-
         ington, D.C.: U.S. Government Printing Office, April 1977); U.S. Bureau of
         the Census, *Historical Statistics of the United States, Colonial Times to
         1970, Bicentennial Edition, Part I* (Washington, D.C.: U.S. Government
         Printing Office, 1975).

EXHIBIT 28
MEDIAN FAMILY INCOME: PRESENCE OF WIFE
IN LABOR FORCE
(in 1974 dollars)

Year	Wife in Paid Labor Force	Wife Not in Paid Labor Force
1950	$ 8,200	$ 6,791
1960	11,490	9,192
1965	13,437	10,303
1970	15,759	11,816
1974	16,928	12,082

SOURCE: Howard Hayghe, "Families and the Rise of Working Wives—An Overview,"
Monthly Labor Review (May 1976):15.

expenditures related to wives in the labor force. Nevertheless, given this level of variation, it is difficult to see the pattern of participation being reversed. Personal expenditure patterns in the United States tend to have a one way ratchet providing for their continual progression. The family making $16,928 (the median family income when wives are in the paid labor force in 1974), would have considerably difficulty, both psychic and fiscal, in moving down to the $12,082 level (the median income for families with wives not in the paid labor force). Assuming that job opportunities continue to expand in quality as well as in number for women, there is little reason to believe that the trends evident here will not continue in the future. And with them, certainly the number of children, desired or practicable, must of necessity be constrained, thus perpetuating the patterns of recent history.

SUMMARY

The primary (husband-wife) family of America, an institution facing increasing challenge from alternative household configurations, is nonetheless gaining economic validity as the nation's citizenry seek to cope with the strictures and opportunities of a more challenging economic and fiscal environment.

1. The pattern of working women, documented earlier, is further accentuated in husband-wife families. Over the past twenty-nine years, the number of working wives (whose husband is present), increased by 208.0 percent; the husband equivalent expanded by only 23.0 percent.

2. The past twenty-six years saw the labor force participation rate of wives increase from 23.8 percent to 45.0 percent. Concurrently, that of husbands contracted from 91.6 percent to 82.1 percent, the statistical complement of changing retirement patterns.

3. Multiple-worker families are becoming the norm in America; by 1975, 48.7 percent, virtually half, of the nation's families had two workers or more. Surprisingly, only in a distinct minority (34.0 percent) was solely the husband employed.

4. The labor force participation rate of wives (husband present) with school-aged children has doubled in the past two and one half decades to definitive majority status (53.7 percent). This broader phenomenon is evident regardless of the realities of childrearing responsibility.

5. Whatever the social and cultural implications for the traditional web of family ties and interrelationships, the economic consequences are manifold. While average weekly earnings have doubled (209.4 percent) during the past twenty-five years, median family incomes have tripled (313.3 percent) over the equivalent span of time.[14]

6. And within the family-defined cohort, the economic implications of multiple workers are equally significant. In 1974, the median income of families with the wife in the paid labor force was $16,928; with the wife absent from the labor force, the median family income fell to $12,082.

7. The very strength of these economic realities generates a net added impetus to the process of household transformation. Certainly, it is paralleled and underscored by the rapid growth within the primary-individual family typology of households comprising unrelated individuals.

8. At the very least, "going it alone" may be economically hazardous. Are we witnessing a fundamental bifurcation in economic capacity between multiple-worker households and their single-worker counterparts, even at equivalent occupational and social status? Will the gap widen if the former secure the protection against inflation and the investment benefits inherent in homeownership?

7

Changing Spatial Distribution: Regional

Spatial redistribution may accentuate or minimize the immediacies of general population growth trends. Areas securing net immigration may be faced with the prospect of educational plant expansion while the nation as a whole experiences substantial contraction of its school-age population—or, at the same time, areas of decline, because of outmigration, may experience an immediate crisis of excess infrastructure. Declining rates of net natural increase thrust migration into an increasingly prominent role in local growth determination. High rates of fertility tend to justify and confirm the vitality of established places, serving to mask the realities of declining areas or at least to obscure the necessity of acknowledging them.[15] As fertility wanes, the positive decisions of people to redistribute themselves—to migrate—become much more apparent and influential. The evolving geography of the nation's population will certainly refine and modify the effects of the parameters and dynamics previously discussed on individual political jurisdictions, and will spawn an array of additional concerns.

The spatial redistribution of America's citizenry, as typified by suburban growth and central city decline in the past two decades, is all too familiar, etched deeply into our day-to-day consciousness. While the history of the United States can be structured in terms of the complex ebbs and flows of migration, until recently, there has been a tendency to overlook the broader, more pervasive, swings in population settlement. The classical analytical works on western expansion, for example, and those concerning the waves of European inmigration that buffeted our cities, dominate the history shelf, with little information to be found on the expansion or contraction of other areas.

The present day equivalent of the areal dimension—the regional dimension—has recently captured the fancy of the popular media, with "Sunbelt" and "Frostbelt" entering the journalists' lexicon and serving as a new reference framework for domestic issues. The principal focus is on the territories being vacated—although some hesitant fascination with the "new South" is evident. This stands in contrast to the primary target of the past historical consciousness, the waves and frontiers of growth. The one major exception was the coverage given to the flight from the land—the great agricultural displacement of the 1930s and more recent periods. In any case, the regional shift, although linked to metropolitan and urban changes, promises to interpenetrate every dimension of national domestic policy and to influence the daily activities of planners and local political leaders, throughout the short-term future.

THE LONGER TERM PATTERNS

As a backdrop to the new concerns of the 1970s, it is useful to examine the patterns of regional change for the two decades prior to 1970, the baseline of the present transformation. Exhibit 29 details the population changes that have taken place on a regional and divisional basis between 1950 and 1970.[16] Between 1950 and 1960, the United States as a whole experienced a rate of growth of 18.5 percent and an absolute increase of 28 million people. The growth was relatively evenly shared (in total numbers) among the major regional clusters, each of which expanded by between 7.2 million and 7.9 million, with the exception of the Northeast, which expanded by only 5.2 million people. Those areas trailing the national growth rate most severely were the industrialized Northeast (13.2 percent) and the agricultural states of the West North Central (9.5 percent) and East South Central (5.0 percent) Divisions. In contrast, the West was the fastest growing area of the nation, increasing in size by 38.9 percent.

Between 1960 and 1970, regional disparities began to come into focus, with the Northeast and North Central Regions differentiated from the South and West. In terms of both absolute growth and percentage change, the former began to lag behind the latter. Indeed, in the face of a shrinking national growth increment (24 million people), the South's net gain in population (7.8 million) was greater than that of the previous decade, thus making it the only region to experience an increasing level of absolute growth. And this growth occurred despite the continued dissolution of labor-intensive farming in the East South Central Division.

THE RECENT ACCELERATION

The trendlines evident in the two decades prior to 1970 foreshadowed the general pattern of events that was to take place in the 1970s, but not its scale and magnitude. A gradual and persistent evolution rapidly accelerated into a process of snowballing momentum. As Exhibit 30 indicates, the 1970 to 1976 growth rate of both the South (9.6 percent) and the West (10.7 percent) was more than ten times greater than that of the Northeast (0.9 percent) and almost

EXHIBIT 29

REGIONAL POPULATION GROWTH PATTERNS: 1950 TO 1970

(numbers in thousands)

Region and Division	1950[1]	1960[2]	1970[3]	Numerical Change		Percentage Change	
				1950–1960	1960–1970	1950–1960	1960–1970
Northeast Region	39,478	44,678	49,061	5,200	4,383	13.2	9.8
New England	9,314	10,509	11,847	1,195	1,338	12.8	12.7
Middle Atlantic	30,164	34,168	37,213	4,004	3,045	13.3	8.9
North Central Region	44,461	51,619	56,593	7,158	4,974	16.1	9.6
East North Central	30,399	36,225	40,266	5,826	4,041	19.2	11.2
West North Central	14,061	15,394	16,328	1,333	934	9.5	6.1
South Region	47,197	54,973	62,812	7,776	7,839	16.5	14.3
South Atlantic	21,182	25,972	30,679	4,790	4,707	22.6	18.1
East South Central	11,477	12,050	12,808	573	758	5.0	6.3
West South Central	14,538	16,951	19,325	2,413	2,374	16.6	14.0
West Region	20,190	28,053	34,838	7,863	6,785	38.9	24.2
Mountain	5,075	6,855	8,290	1,780	1,435	35.1	20.9
Pacific	15,115	21,198	26,549	6,083	5,351	40.2	25.2
U.S. TOTAL	151,326	179,323	203,304	27,997	23,981	18.5	13.4

NOTES:　1. April 1, 1950 Census.
　　　　2. April 1, 1960 Census.
　　　　3. April 1, 1970 Census as reported by source below.

SOURCE:　U.S. Bureau of the Census, *Current Population Reports*, Series P-25, No. 640, "Estimates of the Population of States with Components of Change: 1970 to 1975" (Washington, D.C.: U.S. Government Printing Office, November 1976).

five times greater than that of the North Central Division (2.0 percent). Lagging most severely were the highly industrialized states of the Middle Atlantic and East North Central Divisions, the manufacturing belt of America stretching from New York to Chicago.

The improved relative performance of the West South Central and East South Central Divisions gives some indication that their ranks of rural, former agricultural workers have been depleted, and thus are no longer available to bolster the sagging populations of the northern industrial cities. Also, the former territories have "unloaded" their "redundant" populations thereby setting the stage for improved growth performance.

The energy and natural resources crises of the 1970s improved the economic status of those states that serve as exporters of these vital commodities. Not only is this phenomenon reflected in the growth rate of the southern divisions cited above but also in the Mountain states—whose growth rate (18.6 percent) was the highest in the nation and for the first time eclipsed that of the Pacific Division (8.2 percent)—and the oil-and natural gas-rich territories of the West South Central Division.

Thus, the rise of the Sunbelt and the stagnation of the Northeast and North Central states represent deepening contours on America's population landscape. Exhibit 31 provides an alternative perspective on this development by indicating the shares of national growth secured by each region and division for the three periods under consideration (1950 to 1960, 1960 to 1970, and 1970 to 1976). Again, the data emphasize one of the hazards of forecasting: being right in direction but wrong in time, scale, and dimension. While the earlier data made apparent the shifts in regional growth (at least in hindsight) the future (1976) actually arrived much faster than any but the most omniscient seer could have anticipated. The bulk of the national population growth from 1970 to 1976 was in the province of the South (53.2 percent) and West (32.8 percent). Assuming the most pessimistic stance, it appears that the central city-suburban bifurcation of the past two decades has now been fully amplified to the national scale with the older northern sectors of the country in the central-city role.

THE COMPONENTS OF CHANGE

The declining fertility rates documented previously affect the balance of the two components of population growth—net natural increase and net migration—as it is manifested in each regional territory. Exhibit 32 presents the absolute population change for each region for each five year period between July 1, 1950 and July 1, 1975. (It should be emphasized that for Exhibits 29, 30, and 31 the April 1 benchmark was used for 1970 and prior years.) These increments, while replicating information previously reviewed,

EXHIBIT 30

REGIONAL POPULATION GROWTH PATTERNS: 1970 TO 1976

(numbers in thousands)

Region and Division	1970[1]	1976[2]	Change 1970–1976 Number	Change 1970–1976 Percent	Change 1960–1970 Percent
Northeast Region	49,061	49,503	442	0.9	(9.8)
New England	11,847	12,221	374	3.2	(12.7)
Middle Atlantic	37,213	37,282	69	0.2	(8.9)
North Central Region	56,593	57,739	1,146	2.0	(9.6)
East North Central	40,266	40,934	668	1.7	(11.2)
West North Central	16,328	16,805	477	2.9	(6.1)
South Region	62,812	68,855	6,043	9.6	(14.3)
South Atlantic	30,679	33,990	3,311	10.8	(18.1)
East South Central	12,808	13,661	853	6.7	(6.3)
West South Central	19,325	21,204	1,879	9.7	(14.0)
West Region	34,838	38,562	3,724	10.7	(24.2)
Mountain	8,290	9,833	1,543	18.6	(20.9)
Pacific	26,549	28,729	2,180	8.2	(25.2)
U.S. TOTAL	203,304	214,659	11,355	5.6	(13.4)

NOTES: 1. April 1, 1970 Census as reported in first source below.
2. July 1, 1976 estimate.

SOURCES: U.S. Bureau of the Census, *Current Population Reports,* Series P-25, No. 640, "Estimates of the Population of States with Components of Change: 1970 to 1975" (Washington, D.C.: U.S. Government Printing Office, November 1976); U.S. Bureau of the Census, *Current Population Reports,* Series P-20, No. 307, "Population Profile of the United States: 1976" (Washington, D.C.: U.S. Government Printing Office, April 1977).

provide the base for disaggregation into the components of change, the subject of Exhibit 33.

After reaching its maximum in the 1955 to 1960 period—when the birth rate peaked—population growth due to net natural increase declined in each succeeding five year period in every region, both in terms of absolute size and as a percentage of the population base at the beginning year of each period (see Exhibit 33). At the same time, there has been a tendency for net migration to increase over the past ten years, after the low point reached in the 1960 to 1965 period. Particularly significant is the net inmigration of 2.6 million people (4.1 percent of its July 1970 population) to the South over the past five years; the latter has surpassed the historic magnet (the West) in capturing the bulk of the nation's movers. Indeed, in the space of one generation, the South has evolved from a situation of heavy outmigration losses to very substantial inmigration gains.

EXHIBIT 31
REGION AND DIVISION PERCENTAGE SHARES OF NATIONAL GROWTH
1950 TO 1976

Region and Division	Period 1950–1960	Period 1960–1970	Period 1970–1976
Northeast Region	18.6	18.3	3.9
New England	4.3	5.6	3.3
Middle Atlantic	14.3	12.7	0.6
North Central Region	25.6	20.7	10.1
East North Central	20.8	16.9	5.9
West North Central	4.8	3.9	4.2
South Region	27.8	32.7	53.2
South Atlantic	17.1	19.6	29.2
East South Central	2.0	3.2	7.5
West South Central	8.6	9.9	16.5
West Region	18.1	28.3	32.8
Mountain	6.4	6.0	13.6
Pacific	21.7	22.3	19.2
U.S. TOTAL	100.0	100.0	100.0

SOURCE: Derived from Exhibits 29 and 30.

EXHIBIT 32
POPULATION CHANGE FOR FIVE-YEAR PERIODS BY REGION: 1950 TO 1975
(periods beginning July 1; change expressed in millions)

Period	U.S. Total	Population Change By Region			
		Northeast	North Central	South	West
1950–1955	13.2	2.7	3.9	2.9	3.7
1955–1960	14.9	2.5	3.2	5.0	4.2
1960–1965	13.5	2.6	2.5	4.4	3.9
1965–1970	10.4	1.7	2.4	3.4	2.8
1970–1975	9.3	0.3	1.0	5.1	2.9

SOURCE: U.S. Bureau of the Census, *Current Population Reports,* Series P-25, No.
640, "Estimates of the Population of States with Components of Change:
1970 to 1975" (Washington, D.C.: U.S. Government Printing Office, November 1976).

EXHIBIT 33
POPULATION CHANGE BY COMPONENT BY REGION: FIVE-YEAR PERIODS, 1950 TO 1975
(period beginning July 1; change expressed in millions)

Net Natural Increase

Period	United States	Region Northeast	North Central	South	West
1950–1955	12.1	2.3	3.5	4.5	1.9
1955–1960	13.2	2.6	3.9	4.7	2.2
1960–1965	12.0	2.3	3.3	4.2	2.2
1965–1970	8.7	1.6	2.3	3.0	1.7
1970–1975	6.8	1.0	1.8	2.5	1.5

Percent of Population Base at Beginning Year of Period

Period	United States	Region Northeast	North Central	South	West
1950–1955	8.0	5.9	7.7	9.5	9.1
1955–1960	8.0	6.1	7.9	9.2	9.1
1960–1965	6.7	5.2	6.4	7.5	7.7
1965–1970	4.5	3.4	4.3	5.1	5.3
1970–1975	3.4	2.0	3.2	4.0	4.2

Net Migration

Period	United States	Region Northeast	North Central	South	West
1950–1955	1.0	0.4	0.4	-1.6	1.9
1955–1960	1.7	(Z)	-0.7	0.3	2.0
1960–1965	1.5	0.3	-0.8	0.3	1.7
1965–1970	1.7	0.1	0.1	0.4	1.1
1970–1975	2.5	-0.7	-0.8	2.6	1.4

Percent of Population Base at Beginning Year of Period

Period	United States	Region Northeast	North Central	South	West
1950–1955	0.7	1.0	0.9	-3.5	9.2
1955–1960	1.0	-0.1	-1.3	0.6	8.5
1960–1965	0.8	0.7	-1.6	0.5	6.2
1965–1970	0.9	0.2	0.2	0.7	3.3
1970–1975	1.2	-1.4	-1.5	4.1	4.1

NOTE: 1. Z indicates less than 50,000.

SOURCE: U.S. Bureau of the Census, *Current Population Reports*, Series P-25, No. 640, "Estimates of the Population of States with Components of Change: 1970 to 1975" (Washington, D.C.: U.S. Government Printing Office, November 1976).

EXHIBIT 34
REGION OF RESIDENCE IN MARCH 1970 AND REGION
OF RESIDENCE IN MARCH 1975, FOR MIGRANTS SIXTY-FIVE
YEARS OF AGE AND OVER[1]
(numbers in thousands)[2]

Region of Residence in 1975	Total Migrants	Region of Residence in 1970			
		Northeast	North Central	South	West
United States Total	1,681	422	473	486	299
Northeast	224	202	3	12	7
North Central	344	6	289	29	20
South	744	184	93	427	39
West	369	30	88	18	234
Percent Distribution					
United States Total	100.0	25.1	28.1	28.9	17.8
Northeast	100.0	90.2	1.3	5.4	3.1
North Central	100.0	1.7	84.0	8.4	5.8
South	100.0	24.7	12.5	57.4	5.2
West	100.0	8.1	23.8	4.9	63.4

NOTES: 1. Migrants are all persons who, at the end of the period, were living in a
          county in the United States different from that they lived in at the beginning
          of the period.
          2. Numbers and percents may not sum because of rounding. Percents com-
          puted from rounded data.

SOURCE: U.S. Bureau of the Census, *Current Population Reports,* Series P-20, No.
          285, "Mobility of the Population of the United States: March 1970 to March
          1975" (Washington, D.C.: U.S. Government Printing Office, October 1975).

In the years between 1955 and 1970, the South maintained a slight positive net migration despite the trek north of its rural black population—the terminal shift of population as a function of the agricultural revolution. Only the large influx of people to Florida over this period mitigated the overall migration implications of the latter phenomenon.[17]

Particularly striking in this context is the selective migration of the elderly shown in Exhibit 34. The South was clearly the leading beneficiary of differential interregional shifts while the Northeast and North Central Regions were the major losers. In the former case, from 1970 to 1975, 184,000 elderly individuals (sixty-five years of age and over) migrated from the Northeast to the South with an additional 93,000 migrating from the North Central Region. The skew in origin is reversed when the pattern of inmigration to the West is considered. In this case, 30,000 northeasterners moved to the West while the flow from the North Central Region was nearly triple that, or 88,000.

Conversely, inmigration by elderly people to the Northeast from other regions was relatively trivial (22,000), while the North Central region secured but 55,000 elderly inmigrants. Thus, the patterns of preference are most clear. With early retirement clearly expanding, this type of preferential relocation may take on added significance in the years to come.

Migration is a telling criterion of location shift by choice, of people seeking out "better" places to live. The current preferences of Americans are clearly gauged by the data of Exhibits 33 and 34, with the aging industrial belt being vacated as a matter of conscious choice.

SUMMARY

The secular pattern of population shift in the United States—as exemplified by the advancing western frontier—has been suddenly accentuated. The declining rate and magnitude of net natural increase have increased the import of migration as a source of population growth. And as a matter of affirmative individual decisionmaking, the Sunbelt has gained supremacy as a residential environment of choice.

1. The long term trend (1950 to 1976) showed that the Northeast and North Central states experienced decreasing shares of declining national growth, while the South and West acquired increasing shares of America's population growth, from 55.9 percent in the 1950 to 1960 period, to 61.0 percent over the following decade, to 86.0 percent in the 1970 to 1976 period.

2. This last acceleration promises to be one of the hallmarks of the post-1970 era. From 1970 to 1975, the South and West experienced a net inmigration of 4 million individuals while the Northeast and North Central Regions sustained losses of 1.5 million outmigrants. And the latter indicator may actually underestimate the problems of the aging industrial states, since the United States as a whole experienced a 2.5 million person increase in population because of overseas immigration patterns.[18]

3. Nevertheless, the impetus to flee settings thought of as undesirable socially and environmentally for more attractive alternatives has been expanded to greater spatial scales. Suburban flight has given way to regional shift.

4. Population shifts serve both as signal and as instigator of both economic growth and decline. Certainly, patterns of economic growth and spatial redistribution are highly correlated to the population complement.[19] But, in the context

of population serving economic activity—retailing, for example—population flows foster the rapid replication of deserted facilities, often vacated and wasting as their economic rationale is removed. The fractured landscapes of many declining northern cities bear testimony to the residual effects of population shifts.

5. In the context of the evolving age structure of America's population, which is generating excess capacity in many public facilities and infrastructures—schools, for example—at the aggregate national scale, the sheer magnitude of these population movements implies an endless process of public expenditure in growth territories to replicate the same operations and facilities already existing in vacated territories. And the latter excess facilities are not easily scaled down nor abrogated without adding impetus to the very process of decline.

The regional redistribution of population has other implications that are evident as two intersecting phenomena—metropolitan and nonmetropolitan growth shifts and intrametropolitan patterns of change—are examined.

8

Population Redistribution: Metropolitan, Nonmetropolitan and Intrametropolitan

The basic challenge of contemporary planning activity has been set within the framework of the decline of the central city and the resynthesis of the mainstream of American life in the suburban setting. The intrametropolitan struggles, associated with racial resegregation, fiscal shortfall, infrastructure duplication, and environmental impact, have not as yet shown an appropriate awareness of a broader change of concomitant significance. It is one in which the role of the historic industrial metropolis may soon be coming into question.

Metropolitan-Nonmetropolitan Tensions

For the past half century, the major growth poles of American society were its metropolitan centers. Now, this convention has been relegated to the annals of urban history. As shown in Exhibit 35, the twenty largest metropolitan agglomerations experienced the final stages of their service as the nation's dominant growth loci during the 1960 to 1970 era.[20] Their average annual population increase (1.7 percent) exceeded that of lesser metropolitan places (1.5 percent), and far outdistanced nonmetropolitan territories (0.4 percent).

The threshold changes that have occurred since 1970 are unprecedented in scope. From 1970 to 1974, large metropolitan areas were transformed into settings of slow growth, experiencing an average annual rate of population increase of 0.3 percent. During the same time period, smaller metropolitan areas led the way with an average annual growth rate of 1.5 percent. Yet, the latter are being challenged by the marked resurgence of nonmetropolitan growth, where population increases averaged 1.3 percent annually for the period 1970–1974 (see Exhibit 36). In an equally telling transformation, the twenty largest metropolitan complexes experienced a net migration outflow of 1.2 million people, while nonmetropolitan territories had a net migration inflow of 1.5 million. Some of this shift undoubtedly signifies the drive toward exurbia and can be attributed to the lagging pace of metropolitan definition.[21] However, the latter may be only a secondary explanation for the phenomenon.

The pattern is clarified in Exhibit 36, which partitions metropolitan and nonmetropolitan population growth patterns by regional location. It is the large metropolitan complexes of the Northeast that dominate the post-1970 experience of metropolitan decline, losing 0.3 percent of their population annually. Also exhibiting similar symptoms, although on a lesser plane, are their equivalents in the North Central states, which experienced annual population losses of 0.1 percent. In sharp contrast is the status of large metropolitan areas in the South and West, which demonstrated annual increases of 1.8 and 0.5 percent, respectively.

The major focal points of growth in the Northeast and North Central states are nonmetropolitan areas, which far exceed even the positive growth performances of the smaller metropolitan areas. In the South and West, the bulk of the population growth on an absolute basis is taking place in smaller metropolitan settings. The linkage of regional and metropolitan growth patterns becomes apparent when it is realized that the Northeast has nearly three-fifths of its total population concentrated in four large metropolitan areas. Therefore, the virtual national halt in large metropolitan growth has much greater effect in the Northeast than in the South, where only one-fifth of the population resides in large metropolitan settings. Similarly, the revitalization of the nonmetropolitan sector has negligible positive effects in the Northeast, where only one-seventh of the population is nonmetropolitan; in contrast, the South, where one-third of the population so resides, experiences much greater repercussions from nonmetropolitan growth. Avoiding the question of which shift—regional or metropolitan—is the primary causal factor, we can be certain that their interlinkage is forging a critical dynamic for the immediate future.

When the data for the twenty largest metropolitan agglomerations are further dissected, their losses appear more alarming. As shown in Exhibit 37, every one of the eleven major metropolises in the Northeast and North Central regions experienced net outmigration from 1970 to 1974. Yet, in the South, only Washington, D.C. was similarly afflicted; more than compensating for the latter's performance was the phenomenal growth of Houston, Miami, and Atlanta, clearly indexed by very substantial numbers of inmigrants.

Surprisingly, the West exhibited a pattern similar to the older regions. Los Angeles and Seattle, perhaps subject to the vagaries of the aircraft industry, had negative migration balances while San Francisco's net migration was far below its experience of the preceding decade.

And the losses of the older regions' metropolises are far from trivial. In New York, for example, the net outmigration of 635,000 people represents

EXHIBIT 35

METROPOLITAN AND NONMETROPOLITAN POPULATION CHANGE AND NET MIGRATION: 1960 TO 1974
(population numbers in thousands; migration in millions)

Metropolitan Status[1]	Population			Average Annual Percent Change		Net Migration	
	1960	1970	1974	1960–1970	1970–1974	1960–1970	1970–1974
Total Metropolitan	127,938	149,817	154,964	1.6	0.8	6.4	0.5
Large Metropolitan[2]	69,262	81,471	82,548	1.7	0.3	4.2	-1.2
Other Metropolitan	58,676	68,346	72,416	1.5	1.5	2.2	1.7
Nonmetropolitan	51,373	53,483	56,427	0.4	1.3	-3.2	1.5
Total United States	179,311	203,300	211,391	1.3	1.0	—	—

NOTES: 1. Current metropolitan area definition (1975).
2. Large metropolitan includes areas identified individually in Exhibit 36.

SOURCE: U.S. Bureau of the Census, *Current Population Reports*, Series P-25, No. 640, "Estimates of the Population of States with Components of Change: 1970 to 1975" (Washington, D.C.: U.S. Government Printing Office, 1976).

EXHIBIT 36
POPULATION AND AVERAGE ANNUAL PERCENT CHANGE FOR REGIONS BY METROPOLITAN STATUS: 1960 TO 1974
(numbers in thousands)

Region	Population			Average Annual Percent Change	
	1960	1970	1974	1960–1970	1970–1974
Northeast					
Large Metropolitan	26,309	28,933	28,623	1.0	-0.3
Other Metropolitan	12,300	13,548	13,816	1.3	0.5
Nonmetropolitan	6,069	6,580	6,987	0.8	1.4
North Central					
Large Metropolitan	20,049	22,591	22,559	1.2	-0.1
Other Metropolitan	14,810	16,815	17,226	1.3	0.6
Nonmetropolitan	16,760	17,185	17,759	0.3	0.8
South					
Large Metropolitan	10,232	13,702	14,756	2.9	1.8
Other Metropolitan	22,347	26,112	28,122	1.6	1.7
Nonmetropolitan	22,382	22,998	24,299	0.3	1.3
West					
Large Metropolitan	12,672	16,245	16,610	2.5	0.5
Other Metropolitan	9,219	11,871	13,252	2.5	2.6
Nonmetropolitan	6,162	6,720	7,382	0.9	2.2

NOTE: 1. "Large metropolitan" includes areas identified individually in Exhibit 36. Metropolitan areas as defined in 1975—266 SMSAs.

SOURCE: U.S. Bureau of the Census, *Current Population Reports*, Series P-25, No. 640, "Estimates of the Population of States with Components of Change: 1970 to 1975" (Washington, D.C.: U.S. Government Printing Office, 1976).

EXHIBIT 37

POPULATION AND NET MIGRATION FOR THE TWENTY LARGEST METROPOLITAN AGGLOMERATIONS: 1960 TO 1974[1]

(numbers in thousands)

Region and Area	Population			Change 1960–1970		Change 1970–1974		Net Migration	
	1960	1970	1974	Number	Percent	Number	Percent	1960–1970	1970–1974
Northeast Region									
New York	15,779	17,494	17,181	1,715	10.9	-313	-1.8	301	-635
Philadelphia[2]	5,024	5,628	5,642	604	12.0	14	0.2	98	-105
Boston	3,457	3,849	3,918	392	11.3	69	1.8	61	-2
Pittsburgh	2,405	2,401	2,334	-4	-0.2	-67	-2.8	-166	-89
North Central Region									
Chicago	6,795	7,611	7,615	816	12.0	4	0.0	-6	-242
Detroit	4,122	4,669	4,684	547	13.3	15	0.3	15	-151
Cleveland	2,732	3,000	2,921	268	9.8	-19	-0.6	-36	-159
St. Louis	2,144	2,411	2,371	267	12.5	-40	-1.7	24	-105
Minneapolis-St. Paul	1,598	1,965	2,011	367	23.0	46	2.3	118	-26
Cincinnati[2]	1,468	1,611	1,618	143	9.7	7	0.4	-33	-43
Milwaukee	1,421	1,575	1,589	154	10.8	14	0.9	-29	-30
South Region									
Washington, D.C.	2,097	2,909	3,015	812	38.7	106	3.6	429	-14
Dallas-Ft. Worth	1,738	2,378	2,499	640	36.8	121	5.1	368	10
Houston	1,571	2,169	2,402	598	38.1	233	10.7	328	116
Miami	1,269	1,888	2,223	619	48.8	335	17.7	512	312
Baltimore	1,804	2,071	2,140	267	14.8	69	3.3	54	22
Atlanta	1,169	1,596	1,775	427	36.5	179	11.2	233	102
West Region									
Los Angeles	7,752	9,983	10,231	2,231	28.8	248	2.5	1,172	-84
San Francisco	3,492	4,424	4,585	932	26.7	161	3.6	489	45
Seattle	1,429	1,837	1,794	408	28.6	-43	-2.3	235	-91

NOTES: 1. Standard consolidated statistical areas and standard metropolitan statistical areas (SMSAs).

2. Small portions of Philadelphia and Cincinnati areas are in the South. Thus, regional totals will differ slightly from those in Exhibit 35.

SOURCE: U.S. Bureau of the Census, *Current Population Reports*, Series P-25, No. 640, "Estimates of the Population of States with Components of Change: 1970 to 1975" (Washington, D.C.: U.S. Government Printing Office, 1976).

3.6 percent of its 1970 population, with similar proportions (3.2 percent) moving from Chicago and Detroit. The Cleveland and St. Louis agglomerations fared even worse, experiencing losses of 5.3 and 4.4 percent, respectively. Even the fastest growing metropolitan areas of the Northeast and North Central states, in terms of total population change from 1970 to 1974, are growing at a rate far slower than that of all the southern and western metropolises, except Seattle.

Historically, the sheer growth in population, particularly through migration, generated much of the social and economic stress of our older urban centers. This pattern has changed very markedly, providing both hope and new challenge. The problems of coping with increased housing demand, of overcrowded schools, and overstressed physical facilities may be somewhat alleviated by the new conditions of population stability and decline; but in their place is the question of the fiscal balance—of the economic wherewithal within the older metropolitan settings with which to service the remaining population. This question takes on even more significance as equally important and distressing patterns of change surface inside metropolitan areas.

INTRAMETROPOLITAN SHIFTS

The history of America's major cities is one of meeting—and surmounting—the problems of growth and change. But, for the first time, the nation's central cities in total are losing population, and doing so quite markedly.[22] From 1970 to 1976, their population losses totaled 2.1 million people, or 3.4 percent, while the corresponding suburban rings expanded by 7.7 million people or 10.3 percent (see Exhibit 38). Indeed, while nonmetropolitan growth rates have moved past those of formally defined SMSAs, the suburban rings still represent the fastest growing territories of America, although being pressed hard by nonmetropolitan areas.

Yet, the central cities in total appear in even more difficulty when partitioned by race—they are being vacated by whites at an accelerating pace. The departure by whites represents a net loss of 7.6 percent from 1970 to 1976, almost 3.7 million people (see Exhibit 38). Concurrently, the white-population gains (6.1 million) of the suburban rings were almost twice the central-city loss.

In contrast, stands the black population growth increment within central cities and suburban rings—its numbers increased by 1.5 million in each. Hence, only between one-third and one-half of the loss of whites within America's cities was offset by black increases. The pattern shown in Exhibit 38 documents the momentum of black suburbanization. While the central city and suburban growth totals are virtually equivalent, the 36.3 percentage change in the latter indicates the basic pattern of choice and preference. A partial vacuum is therefore opening up in the central cities, given both the

EXHIBIT 38

POPULATION OF THE UNITED STATES BY METROPOLITAN AND NONMETROPOLITAN RESIDENCE AND RACE: 1976 AND 1970

(numbers in thousands)

Race and Residence	1970[1]	1976[2]	Change 1970 to 1976	Percent Change 1960 to 1970[3]	Percent Change 1970 to 1976	Average Annual Percent Change 1960 to 1970[3]	Average Annual Percent Change 1970 to 1976[4]
All races	199,819	210,332	10,513	13.3	5.3	1.3	0.9
Metropolitan areas[5]	137,058	142,567	5,509	16.6	4.0	1.5	0.7
In central cities[6]	62,876	60,730	-2,146	6.5	-3.4	0.6	-0.6
Outside central cities	74,182	81,837	7,655	26.7	10.3	2.4	1.6
Nonmetropolitan areas	62,761	67,765	5,004	6.8	8.2	0.7	1.3
White	175,276	182,638	7,362	11.9	4.2	1.1	0.7
Metropolitan areas[5]	118,938	121,392	2,454	14.0	2.1	1.3	0.3
In central cities[6]	48,909	45,215	-3,694	0.1	-7.6	—	-1.2
Outside central cities	70,029	76,177	6,148	26.1	8.8	2.3	1.4
Nonmetropolitan areas	56,338	61,246	4,908	7.8	8.7	0.8	1.4
Black and other races	24,453	27,694	3,151	24.3	12.8	2.2	2.0
Metropolitan areas[5]	18,120	21,175	3,055	36.9	16.9	3.1	2.5
In central cities[6]	13,967	15,515	1,548	36.5	11.1	3.1	1.7
Outside central cities	4,153	5,660	1,507	38.1	36.3	3.2	5.2
Nonmetropolitan areas	6,423	6,519	96	-1.6	1.5	-0.2	0.2

NOTES:

1. For comparability with data from the Current Population Survey, figures from the 1970 census have been adjusted to exclude inmates of institutions and members of the Armed Forces living in barracks and similar types of quarters.
2. Five-quarter annual averages centered on April from the Current Population Survey.
3. Based on total 1970 and 1960 census populations, including the categories not covered in the Current Population Survey.
4. Based on the method of exponential change.
5. Population of the 243 standard metropolitan statistical areas (SMSAs) as defined in 1970 census publications.
6. 1976 data for the central cities refer to their January 1, 1970 boundaries and exclude areas annexed since 1970.

SOURCE: U.S. Bureau of the Census, *Current Population Reports*, Series P-20, No. 307, "Population Profile of the United States: 1976" (Washington, D.C.: U.S. Government Printing Office, April 1977).

EXHIBIT 39
POPULATION CHANGE, SELECTED CITIES: 1950 TO 1975

City	1950[1]	1970[2]	1975[3]	Change: 1950–1975 Number	Change: 1950–1975 Percent	Change: 1970–1975 Number	Change: 1970–1975 Percent
Boston	801,444	641,071	636,725	-164,719	-20.6	-4,346	-0.7
Buffalo	580,132	462,768	407,160	-172,972	-29.8	-55,068	-12.0
Chicago	3,620,962	3,366,957	3,099,391	-521,571	-14.4	-267,566	-7.9
Cincinnati	503,998	452,524	412,564	-51,474	-10.2	-39,960	-8.8
Cleveland	914,808	750,903	638,793	-276,015	-30.2	-112,110	-14.9
Detroit	1,849,568	1,511,482	1,335,085	-514,483	-27.8	-176,397	-11.7
Minneapolis	521,718	434,400	378,112	-143,606	-27.5	-56,288	-13.0
New York City	7,891,957	7,894,862	7,481,613	-410,344	-5.2	-413,249	-5.2
Newark	438,776	382,417	339,568	-99,208	-22.6	-42,849	-11.2
Philadelphia	2,071,605	1,948,609	1,815,808	-255,797	-12.3	-132,801	-6.8
Pittsburgh	676,806	520,117	458,651	-218,155	-32.2	-61,466	-11.8
St. Louis	856,796	622,236	524,964	-331,832	-38.7	-97,272	-15.6

NOTES: 1. April 1, 1950 Census.
2. April 1, 1970 Census.
3. July 1, 1975 Population Estimate.

SOURCES: U.S. Bureau of the Census, *County and City Data Book, 1956* (A Statistical Abstract Supplement) (Washington, D.C.: U.S. Government Printing Office, 1957); U.S. Bureau of the Census, *County and City Data Book, 1967* (A Statistical Abstract Supplement) (Washington, D.C.: U.S. Government Printing Office, 1967); U.S. Bureau of the Census, *Census of Population: 1970* Vol. 1, "Characteristics of the Population, Part 1, United States Summary—Section 1" (Washington, D.C.: U.S. Government Printing Office, 1973); U.S. Bureau of the Census, *Current Population Reports: Population Estimates and Projections*, Series P-25 (various state report numbers) (Washington, D.C.: U.S. Government Printing Office, 1977).

lagging pace of natural increase and the pattern of net outmigration.

Despite the confusion that may be caused by introducing yet another terminal date for a data series, the longer term pattern for select individual cities is of great relevance. Exhibit 39 highlights the sheer magnitude of the declines registered by a number of the nation's major cities over the 1950 to 1975 period.

The losses are startling, with St. Louis having the dubious honor of the greatest rate of decline, 38.7 percent. And, for almost all of the observations, except Boston, the 1970 to 1975 changes represent an acceleration of long-term trendlines.

As hypothesized earlier, the emerging household formations of America are of a format that is at least susceptible to having urban preferences, i.e., a diminished necessity for securing ideal child-rearing environments. Whatever tentative stirrings exist for a back-to-the-city movement, their overall impact must be tempered by the sheer magnitude of the declines documented in Exhibit 39.

SUMMARY

The post-1970 era requires a basic reference-framework alteration, not only to account for an increasing regional presence but also to recognize the emergence of nonmetropolitan places as major growth loci. Indeed, nowhere are the conventions of the past more sternly challenged than in the new experience of declining metropolitan areas.

1. From 1970 to 1976, metropolitan areas in total (243 SMSAs) experienced a growth rate of 4.0 percent. In contrast, nonmetropolitan areas had an 8.2 percent increase in population, a reversal of what had long been considered conventional wisdom.

2. The large metropolitan agglomerations of the Northeast and North Central Regions led this reversal, experiencing absolute population declines over the 1970 to 1974 period. Virtually all of them experienced net outmigration during this period. The future role of the traditional industrial metropolis is increasingly coming into question.

3. Similarly, America's central cities in total for the first time (1970 to 1976) lost population, and did so quite markedly. The pattern of white losses evolved from the no-growth status of the preceding decade. In contrast, the rate of increase of blacks and other races in central cities plummeted.

4. At the same time, black suburbanization is rapidly increasing. The number of blacks residing in suburbia increased by 36.3 percent in the past six years.

5. As a result, America's largest central cities have experienced an acceleration of their rate of population loss within the past twenty-five years. For example, by 1975, St. Louis' 1950 population level had declined by 38.7 percent, Pittsburgh's by 32.2 percent, Cleveland's by 30.2 percent, and Buffalo's by 29.8 percent.

6. The implications of these shifts are manifold. To cite one example, the problem of the central city may no longer be the stimulation of additions to the housing stock, but rather the provision of take-out mechanisms for those units no longer required by a shrinking population. While the issue may be offset temporarily by continued contraction in household sizes, to view problems such as residential abandonment in the abstract, without studying the broader population shifts, is to do these problems less than justice.

7. Finally, it is interesting to speculate further on the housing-demand question. Our main repositories of multifamily dwellings—the cities—are actively shrinking, while the settings of single-family dominance—nonmetropolitan areas—are booming. The presence of multifamily dwellings in suburbia notwithstanding, does this growth give some indication of basic choice and preference? In this context, it is interesting to note that the tentative stirrings of a back-to-the-city movement are often associated with a rationale predicated on the quality of older single-family dwellings extant in urban areas.

CONCLUSION

Quietly and persistently, America's population is enmeshed in the throes of change. While not as dramatic as the sporadic social outbursts of the 1960s nor, for that matter, as engrossing to the media as the current energy-related issues, this evolution gives every indication of being a critical determinant of the future course of the nation. The questions are many and the answers few; nonetheless, the broader outlines reviewed here promise to intersect the immediacies faced by planners and policymakers in their day-to-day activities. Critical local issues and questions will be underscored by the broader forces we have tried to specify. While these forces must be elaborated in scope and depth, their initial reference framework is one which cannot be ignored.

Notes

1. "While the total population has increased throughout American history, the rate of growth has undergone a long term decline with the only major interruption being due to the "baby boom" following the Second World War. During the first half of the 19th century, the population of the United States increased at an average rate of about 3 percent per year. Subsequently, the growth rate dropped, largely because of a pronounced decline in fertility, to an average of 0.7 percent per year during the 1930s. The annual growth rate then increased to 1.7 percent during the 1950s at the peak of the baby boom before declining again to the current level, which is about equal to the historically low rate of the 1930s." U.S. Bureau of the Census, *Current Population Reports,* Series P-25, No. 704, "Projections of the Population of the United States: 1977 to 2050" (Washington, D.C.: U.S. Government Printing Office, July 1977) pp. 4-5.

2. The reader is cautioned on the January 1 benchmark of Exhibits 1 and 2. Since projection and estimation dates vary from the traditional April 1 base of the decennial census, care should be exercised in any tabular comparisons. July 1 usually marks the beginning of the estimation and projection periods.
3. The estimated 1974 population of France was 52.5 million; West Germany, 62.0 million; and Japan, 109.7 million. *The World Almanac 1976* (New York: Newspaper Enterprise Association, Inc., 1975).
4. See: U.S. Bureau of the Census, *Current Population Reports,* Series P-20, No. 307. "Population Profile of the United States:1976" (Washington, D.C.: U.S. Government Printing Office, April 1977).
5. There are a number of measures which gauge the role of births in population change (natility) and/or actual birth performance (fertility). The following is a highly simplified presentation of the basic indicators, secured from Henry S. Shryock, Jacob S. Siegel, and Associates, *The Methods and Materials of Demography,* Third Printing, rev., Publication of the U.S. Bureau of the Census (Washington, D.C.: U.S. Government Printing Office, 1975). The simplest and most common measure of fertility is the *total* or *crude birth rate,* defined as the number of births occurring in a year per 1,000 midyear population, that is:

$$\frac{B}{P} \times 1000$$

This measure is used in Exhibit 18 to describe the long-term secular pattern of birth rates. It is useful in indicating directly the influence of natility to the overall population growth rate; however, it is limited analytically because it is influenced by the specific age–sex composition of a population, i.e., the total birth rate may rise or fall simply as a function of the changing size of the childbearing age cohorts, for example.

Age specific birth rates are also commonly employed. An age specific birth rate is defined as the number of births to women of a given age group per 1000 women in that age group. For example, the rate attendant to women of 20 to 24 years of age is:

$$\frac{B_{20-24}}{P^f_{20-24}} \times 1000$$

This measure thus is unaffected by age structure variation and is useful, for example, in elaborating long term trendlines or cross-sectional comparisons.

Another overall age-limited measure is the *general fertility rate,* defined as the number of births per 1000 women of childbearing age. Typically, the total number of births is employed in the numerator and the female population 15 to 44 years of age in the denominator:

$$\frac{B}{P^f_{15-44}} \times 1000$$

The *total fertility rate* is the sum of the age-specific birth rates of women over their reproductive span, as observed in a given year. Hence, it is an age–sex adjusted measure of fertility that takes account of age detail within the childbearing ages. It is defined as:

$$\sum_{x=15}^{44} \frac{B_x}{P_x} \times 1000$$

The total fertility rate gives the number of births 1,000 women would have if they experienced a given set of age-specific birth rates throughout their reproductive span. It can also be interpreted as representing the completed fertility of a synthetic cohort of women.

6. The Census Bureau considers the Series II projection to be its best estimate, with the assumed level of future fertility corresponding closely to that suggested by recent survey data (see Exhibit 16). The fertility assumptions of Series I and Series III were chosen by the Bureau to provide a range that appears likely to encompass future fertility. See: U.S. Bureau of the Census, *Current Population Reports,* Series P–20, No. 308, "Fertility of American Women:June 1976" (Washington, D.C.: U.S. Government Printing Office, 1977).

7. U.S. Bureau of the Census, *Current Population Reports,* Series P–25, No. 704, "Projections of the Population of the United States:1977 to 2050" (Washington, D.C.: U.S. Government Printing Office, July 1977).

8. Editors, "The Graying of the Soft-Drink Industry" *Business Week* (May 23, 1977):68.

9. U.S. Bureau of the Census, *Current Population Reports,* Series P–20, No. 307, "Population Profile of the United States:1976" (Washington, D.C.: U.S. Government Printing Office, April 1977). See also: U.S. Bureau of the Census, *Current Population Reports,* Series P–20, No. 309, "School Enrollment—Social and Economic Characteristics of Students:October 1976" (Washington, D.C.: U.S. Government Printing Office, July 1977).

10. The import of this contraction for planning related analyses cannot be ignored. For example, the traditional intercensal population estimation procedure used by many small political units is usually premised on a base level (census count) figure to which additions in succeeding years are a function of net increments of dwelling units multiplied by various average household-size multipliers. While shrinking household sizes obviously have a direct impact on the shape of the latter, their effect on the base level population is often ignored. If we conceptualize the base as a fixed stock of dwelling units occupied by households, rather than as a total population level per se, then to assume that the population base is fixed in such methodological procedures is dubious. The internal dynamics of the existing stock of dwellings will also reflect household-size changes.

11. The following discussions of recent fertility-rate trends are significant in this regard: June Sklar and Beth Berkov, "The American Birth Rate:Evidences of a Coming Rise," *Science* Vol. 189, No. 4204 (August 29, 1975): 693-700; Campbell Gibson, "The U.S. Fertility Decline, 1961–1975:The Contribution of Changes in Marital Status and Marital Fertility," *Family Planning Perspectives* Vol. 8, No. 5 (September/October 1976):249-252; Campbell Gibson, "The Elusive Rise in the American Birth Rate," *Science* Vol. 196, No. 4289 (April 29, 1977):500-503.

12. In the future, the more general availability of tests of fetal abnormality, which tends to be coupled to elderly primiparas, may make even this prediction hazardous. The

dangers involved for both mother and child in elderly childbirth will be greatly mitigated.

13. Labor force and employment statistics are derived from the Current Population Survey (CPS) undertaken by the Bureau of the Census. The Bureau of Labor Statistics (U.S., Department of Labor) has the responsibility for analyzing and publishing CPS labor force data. The following definitions are relevant to the discussion in the text:

    Labor Force. The civilian labor force comprises the total of all civilians (noninstitutionalized, sixteen years of age and over) classified as employed and unemployed. The total labor force, in addition, includes members of the Armed Forces stationed either in the United States or abroad.

    Employment. Employed persons comprise (1) all those who, during the survey week, did any work at all as paid employees, or in their own business, profession, or on their own farm, or who worked fifteen hours or more as unpaid workers in a family-operated enterprise; (2) all those who did not work but had jobs or businesses from which they were temporarily absent due to illness, bad weather, vacation, labor-management dispute, or various personal reasons—whether or not they were seeking other jobs. Each employed person is counted only once.

    Unemployment. Unemployed persons include those who did not work at all during the survey week, were looking for work, and were available for work during the reference period except for temporary illness.

    Participation Rate. This rate represents the proportion of the noninstitution population (sixteen years of age and over) that is in the labor force (either civilian labor force or total labor force). See: U.S., Department of Labor, Bureau of Labor Statistics, *BLS Handbook of Methods for Surveys and Studies* Bulletin 1910 (Washington, D.C.: U.S. Government Printing Office, 1976) pp. 5-7.

14. Again the implications for professional-related planning analyses are significant. The growing differential and the absolute magnitude of the difference between worker's earnings and family income must be considered in any attempt to specify future housing demand, particularly with respect to the low- and moderate-income sector. With an increasing proportion of wives working, a problematical determination will be the changing proportion of families with incomes defined as low and moderate. Certainly, trends in worker earnings may not be an adequate basis from which to extrapolate housing cost-income relationships.

15. For a discussion of this point, see: Wilbur R. Thompson, "Aging Industries and Cities: Time and Tides in the Northeast" in George Sternlieb and James W. Hughes, eds., *Revitalizing the Northeast: A Prelude to an Agenda* (New Brunswick, N.J.: Rutgers University Center for Urban Policy Research, 1977).

16. The composition of the regions and divisions is as follows:

NORTHEAST REGION

Middle Atlantic Division	New England Division	
New York	Maine	Massachusetts
New Jersey	New Hampshire	Rhode Island
Pennsylvania	Vermont	Connecticut

NORTH CENTRAL REGION

East North Central Division		West North Central Division	
Ohio	Michigan	Minnesota	So. Dakota
Indiana	Wisconsin	Iowa	Nebraska
Illinois		Missouri	Kansas
		No. Dakota	

SOUTH REGION

South Atlantic Division	East South Central Division	West South Central Division
Delaware	Kentucky	Arkansas
Maryland	Tennessee	Louisiana
Dist. of Columbia	Alabama	Oklahoma
Virginia	Mississippi	Texas
West Virginia		
No. Carolina		
So. Carolina		
Georgia		
Florida		

WEST REGION

Mountain Division		Pacific Division
Montana	New Mexico	Washington
Idaho	Arizona	Oregon
Wyoming	Utah	California
Colorado	Nevada	Hawaii
		Alaska

17. U.S. Bureau of the Census, *Current Population Reports,* Series P–25, No. 640, "Estimates of the Population of States with Components of Change:1970 to 1975" (Washington, D.C.: U.S. Government Printing Office, November 1976), p. 2.

18. For example, if the Northeast received 1 million overseas immigrants from 1970 to 1975 (hypothetical), and yet had a net outmigration of 700,000 people (actual), then the actual net outmigration was 1.7 million people (not considering overseas replacements).

19. For a summary of interregional job shifts, see: George Sternlieb and James W. Hughes, "New Metropolitan and Regional Realities of America," *Journal of the American Institute of Planners* Vol. 43, No. 3 (July 1977):227-241.

20. The term agglomeration is used since metropolitan status in this context includes standard consolidated statistical areas.

21. This can be seen by examining the pre- and post-1970 migration shifts of the 243

SMSAs as they were defined at the time of the 1970 census (these SMSAs do not include new ones that have been created since 1970 nor counties added since then to the SMSAs existing in 1970).

METROPOLITAN MIGRATION:
1965 TO 1970 AND 1970
TO 1975

Migration	1965 to 1970	1970 to 1975
Net Migration	+ 352,133	−1,594,000
Inmigration	+5,809,415	+5,127,000
Outmigration	−5,457,282	−6,721,000

See: U.S. Bureau of the Census, *Current Population Reports,* Series P–20, No. 285, "Mobility of the Population of the United States:March 1970, March 1975" (Washington, D.C.: U.S. Government Printing Office, October 1975).
22. Migration again accentuates the overall pattern. Between March 1975 and March 1976, central cities lost 4.6 million persons and gained only 2.7 million persons through migration, for a net loss of 1.9 million. See: U.S. Bureau of the Census, *Current Population Reports,* Series P–20, No. 305, "Geographical Mobility:March 1975 to March 1976" (Washington, D.C.: U.S. Government Printing Office, January 1977).